Featured on ABC-TV'S GOOD MORNING AMERICA!

"Best of the latest special-interest offerings. A first-rate general resource." *US News & World Report.*

"A good book for families seeking alternatives to theme parks and expensive hotels." *Backpacker Magazine.*

"The experiences of the respondents will be of timeless interest and use. Recommended for most travel collections." *Library Journal.*

"Impressively detailed, with many creative ideas, a bible of sorts when it comes to planning a family vacation." *Litchfield County Times.*

"Hot off the press, FAMILY TRAVEL gives a nice overview of various non-traditional family vacation possibilities." *Family Travel Times.*

"The ideas are all unique and affordable: rain forests in Costa Rica, dinosaur tracks in Colorado, rafting, skiing, even house exchange." *South Florida Parenting.*

"A fine book for a family to dream over as they plan their next vacation. Well-designed book has an open format and is profusely illustrated with antique etchings." *Travelwriter Marketletter.*

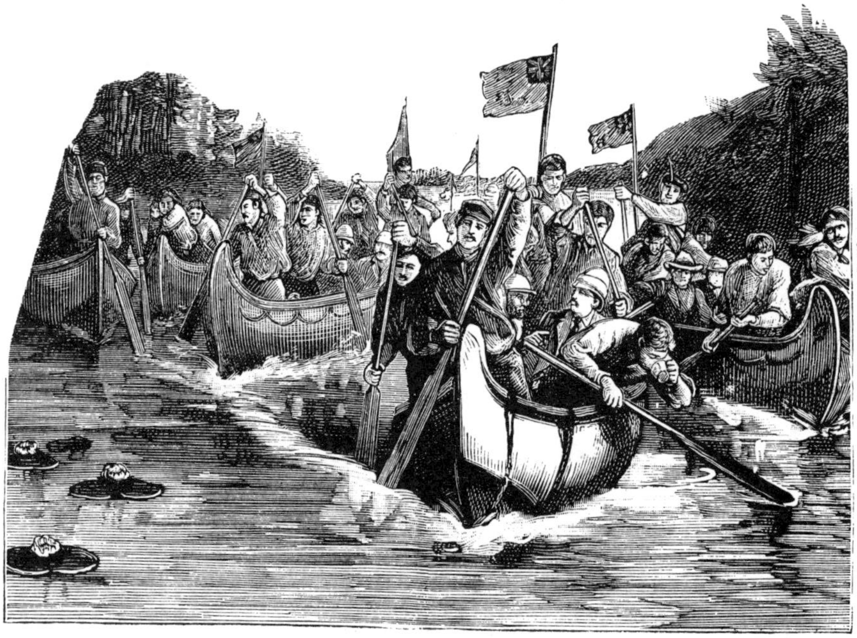

FAMILY TRAVEL

TERRIFIC NEW VACATIONS FOR TODAY'S FAMILIES

BY **EVELYN KAYE**

AUTHOR OF THE AWARD-WINNING "TRAVEL AND LEARN"

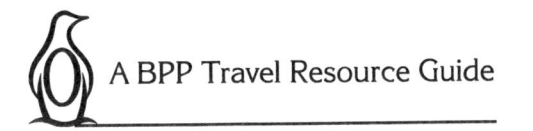

A BPP Travel Resource Guide

Family Travel
Terrific New Vacations for Today's Families
by Evelyn Kaye

Published by Blue Penguin Publications
3031 Fifth Street
Boulder, CO 80304

All rights reserved. No part of this book may be reproduced or transmitted in any form or by any means, electronic or mechanical including photocopying, recording or by any information storage or retrieval system without written permission from the publisher, except for the inclusion of brief quotations in a review.

Every effort has been made to make sure that the information in this book is accurate, but the world of travel is constantly changing. The publisher takes no responsibility for inaccuracies relating to the material included.

Cover photo: Flatirons III by R. L. Castellino
Cover design: Concepts 3

FAMILY TRAVEL was designed on PageMaker® 4.0 for Windows. *Katrina*, *Hot Air*, and *Wright* Typecase™ fonts from Glyphix were used. The book was printed on recycled paper.

© Copyright 1993 by Evelyn Kaye

First Edition
Printed in the United States of America

Library of Congress No: 93-09008

ISBN 0-9626231-3-X

CONTENTS

THANKS AND ACKNOWLEDGEMENTS

1 NEW FAMILY VACATIONS
Introduction. How family vacations have changed; budget, preparations, and the range of options available today.

9 TRAVEL TIPS
Advice on airplane trips; ideas on what to bring.

13 ABOUT THIS BOOK
How to use a Travel Resource Guide, where to find what you want, definitions explained.

17 DOWN ON THE FARM
Farm life, preparations, what to ask a farmer, with children. Resource guide to farms.

29 CAMPING IN THE OPEN
What to expect, family experiences, equipment to consider, tent camping, car camping, checklists.

41 ECO-VACATIONS
Environmental and nature trips in US and abroad. Resource guide to trips.

55 NO-COST LOW-COST VACATIONS
Free vacations in parks, service positions, what to ask, with children, be prepared. Resource guide.

73 ON FOOT AND ON WHEELS
What you need for dayhikes, backpacking, biking, equipment list, with children, be prepared. Resource guide to hiking and biking trips.

97 YOUR HOUSE IS MY HOUSE
House exchanges, homestays, and rentals, in US and abroad. Resource guide to groups and directories.

111 OVER THE SEAS AND FAR AWAY
Group family trips or on your own to Europe, Asia, Australia, and more. Resource guide to trips abroad.

123 RANCHES AND COWBOYS
Dude ranches and cattle round-ups, what to bring, questions to ask, with children. Resource guide to ranches. List of 40 Colorado ranches.

139 SKI AND SNOW
Where to go, what to ask, what's free for children. Resource Guide to skiing in US and Europe.

151 TRAVEL AND LEARN
Study the arts, American Indian culture, dinosaurs. Travel with grandparents, with children, be prepared. Resource guide.

167 ON THE WATER
Family trips on houseboats, river rafts, canoes and kayaks. What to take, checklist, with children. Resource guide.

187 BIBLIOGRAPHY

189 RESOURCE DIRECTORY
Vacations for Children
　Babies and Toddlers
　5 to 12 year olds
　Teenagers
Camping Directory
US State Tourist Offices
Volunteer Openings

198 INDEX

THE AUTHOR

As a child, Evelyn Kaye traveled to Canada from England with her grandmother and ended up staying in Toronto for four years. She's traveled ever since, with her family and on her own. After school in England, she spent a year in Paris, and a year living in Jerusalem. She has explored Italy, Sicily, Denmark, Sweden, Belgium, the Netherlands, Switzerland, Ecuador, Australia, New Zealand, and India. She's sailed round the Galapagos Islands, camped in an Amazon rainforest, rafted through the Grand Canyon, collected shells on Florida's Sanibel Island, hiked in New Hampshire's White Mountains. She can also find her way around New York City, Chicago, Los Angeles, San Francisco, Denver, Washington DC, and Boston.

A journalist in England, she was the first woman reporter in the *Manchester Guardian*'s newsroom, and in France was a reporter for Reuters News Agency. In the United States, she has had articles published in the *New York Times* and *Boston Globe* as well as in *McCalls, Travel & Leisure, Glamour, Ladies Home Journal,* and other major publications.

Among her 14 books is the award-winning *"Travel and Learn: The New Guide to Educational Travel," "Eco-Vacations: Enjoy Yourself and Save the Earth," "How to Treat TV With TLC," "College Bound,"* and *"The Family Guide to Cape Cod."* She is co-author of a college textbook, *"Relationships in Marriage and the Family."*

A past president of the American Society of Journalists and Authors, she is a member of the North American Travel Journalists Association, and president of Colorado Independent Publishers Association. She is listed in *Who's Who in America*.

THANKS AND ACKNOWLEDGEMENTS

Writing this book has been a truly enjoyable experience because I've learned about so many great family vacations. I sent questionnaires and letters out to more than 100 people asking them to describe their favorite family vacations in as much detail as they could remember.

There was a terrific response! Looking back at good times is fun, and I loved listening to the details, so it made for entertaining letters and enjoyable telephone conversations.

When companies and trips were recommended, I asked them for names of recent participants and comments. My thanks to the dozens of organizations who provided materials and information, and to those who provided enthusiastic letters and phone interviews.

Special thanks to Claire Walter who wrote the chapter on family skiing (an activity I've never tried) and lent me stacks of travel clips from her voluminous files. Thanks also to Laura Caruso for copy-editing and proofreading, and to Kathryn Black who read the manuscript as a parent of young children, and gave me her expert reactions.

Other friends were generous in sharing their experiences. My thanks to Lillian Ambrosino, Linda Cornett, Janet Gardner, Carol Gibbon, Reed Glenn, Toni Goldfarb, Lois Libien, Pamela Novotny, Bob Rogers, and Grace Weinstein. In addition, my warm appreciation to the Boulder Media Women whose Friday morning camaraderie is always appreciated, and the committee of the Colorado Independent Publishers Association for their savvy advice on designers and printers.

Personal vacation experiences brought back many happy memories. As a family, we've tried horse riding at a Colorado dude ranch, toured England in a freezing December, paddled a canoe on a peaceful Cape Cod pond, hiked in the rain in Vermont, ordered breakfast in a Paris restaurant, taken the train from Denver to California, picked oranges off the trees in Florida, and climbed to the top of Maine's Mount Cadillac.

My family will recognize the vacations they've enjoyed—and endured—with me. My thanks and appreciation to Katrina and Nick, David and Lisa, and Claire and Spencer, who haven't taken too many vacations yet.

A special and immeasurable thank-you to my Blue Penguin partner Christopher Sarson. He's taken the trips with me, kept calm in the crises, waited out the storms, and kept the project on track. Together we designed and created this book on our mutually compatible computers, and, yes, here's to the next one.

NEW FAMILY VACATIONS

Ever dreamed of taking a perfect family vacation? Imagine—you, and those you love and care about the most, will go somewhere absolutely wonderful. When you get there, every problem is solved, the weather is perfect, you smile the whole time, and each day is more delightful than the one before.

Well, it's not easy to fill those specifications. But it is possible. Finding a great vacation for today's families takes research, planning, creativity, and a sense of adventure, but it can be done. In fact, it may be easier today than it ever was.

Families traveling on vacation today are different from the families of yesterday. Most parents are working at outside jobs so free time is doubly precious. They live with tight budget limitations so they want good value for their vacation. And they want an experience everyone will enjoy.

Today, too, there aren't as many two-parent-two-child stereotypes as in the past. You find single parents planning vacations with friends, step-families and divorced parents coping with children from different marriages, older parents discovering new family vacations, and grandparents traveling with grandchildren.

DIVIDE TO SURVIVE
"I think that people traveling by car with children would do well to have plexiglass installed between the front and back seats. That way, when the kids argue about whose knee is impinging upon whose side, you can't hear them. You think I'm kidding..."

A parent.

2 FAMILY TRAVEL

OFF-SEASON DELIGHTS
"We went to England in winter so the rates were low, and rented an apartment in London. It snowed, and everything looked so pretty!"
Mother, after trip with 12-year-old daughter.

A survey by the National Tour Association showed that more than two-thirds of Americans older than 50 wanted to travel with members of other generations.

Changes in Travel

Today's families don't take long vacations. Statistics show that most families choose shorter breaks but take them more frequently. They go away for a week or a long weekend two or three times a year instead of a month in the summer. They prefer unusual locations rather than established vacation resorts. They choose educational trips where they can benefit from the trip. They look for activities like river rafting, canoeing, and biking. Most important, they enjoy bringing their children along and want them to share the experience.

The world of travel is responding to the waves of change. Some hotel chains offer day-care and children's programs. Resorts provide day camps with activities for children of different ages. Club Med, once a center for swinging couples, welcomes families with Mini-Club activities for children aged 2 to 11. Cruise ships find space for nurseries, children's programs, and teenage activities. Ski resorts have expanded their programs for youngsters. Hiking groups create family treks designed for parents and children. Adventure travel companies offer family excursions to Africa, Australia, and Asia.

New Places to Go

This expansion opens up new and fascinating ideas for family vacations. You can explore a tropical rainforest in Costa Rica to gaze at dazzling blue butterflies and brightly colored macaws and stay in a jungle lodge with hammocks swinging on the veranda. You can visit Nepal and trek through the magnifi-

NEW FAMILY VACATIONS 3

BEST TRIP
"Taking our children to the rainforest with a guide who could answer their questions was one of the best things we ever did."
Parents after Costa Rica trip

cent scenery of the Himalayas, the highest mountains in the world, or fly to Africa, and join a safari in Tanzania specially geared to children and families. You can swap your home for a palazzo in Venice, a condominium in Aspen, a beachfront estate in Florida, a castle in Ireland. You can rent an apartment in London to live like the locals do.

Closer to home, you can take a canoe trip in the pristine waters of the Minnesota lakes region, and catch fish that you cook for dinner. Try river-rafting through the canyons of the west and sleep under the stars. Tune into the easy-going pace of life on a farm in Pennsylvania, where the food is fresh-picked and the evenings are peaceful. Bike trips take you pedalling through small towns and along deserted side roads, and you can pedal a tandem made for two in the mountain scenery of Colorado. Leisurely hiking trips let you walk while the llamas or burros carry the baggage, or take toddler hikes with very young children.

A winter excursion at a ski resort provides activity for all the family and time for parents to be on their own. You can even find free vacations in exchange for your services; you camp for free in a Florida state park and serve as a campground host, greeting people, answering questions, and leading nature walks.

PLAN AHEAD
"The year my parents took us to Europe, we talked about it for weeks, and planned the route we would take and what we would see. It made everything much more interesting when we were traveling."
High School Student.

Plan Ahead

The secret of a successful family vacation is one simple word: preparation.

The best family vacations fall into place after careful planning. Spur-of-the-moment escapes may work for single travelers who can fly away instantly. For families taking off, it's worth spending time to plan it first.

Research the Options: Most travel agents are geared to booking vacations with major hotels and resorts. It may take

4 FAMILY TRAVEL

DO YOUR OWN THING
A parent recommends: "If you go to a place with lots of different activities, each person can merrily go and do his or her own thing, and then you can gather for lunch or drinks or dinner or whatever. There's just enough togetherness but not too much."

research to go camping, take an environmental trip, or explore a national park.

A Connecticut father wanted to spend a week with his son on a small Caribbean island with no casinos or fancy hotels. "Travel agents didn't know what I wanted, so I ended up making all the arrangements myself. It cost less than booking through a travel agency," he noted, "but it took a lot of time."

Talk It Through: Talk to your partner or other adults coming along on the vacation. If your children are old enough, include them in the discussion. Get everyone together, and spend a little time talking about what you'd like to do. Let everyone see the brochures, study the maps, read a travel book, and consider different possibilities. Keep it relaxed and informal, make it clear you're in charge, but be ready to listen. Call absent family members to tell them the plans. Your sister may suggest some good ideas if you ask for them.

Consider Who's Coming: A toddler is very different from a 10-year-old, and a 12-year-old is almost grown-up compared to a 6-year-old. Are the adults compatible? Do you get on with your mother, his parents, your sister-in-law? Will you be traveling with a new baby? Is this the year your son is home all summer while your ex-spouse goes to Australia? Do you need your teenage babysitter along to help with the children?

Analyze the Activities: Are you a gung-ho active bunch of joggers and swimmers and tennis players? Are you a laid-back group who'd prefer to lie in a hammock with a good mystery? Think about what your family most enjoys right now, depending on their ages, interests and abilities. Do your vacations include nightlife, restaurants, cafes, museums, and entertainment? Or do you long to get away from it all to somewhere peaceful and isolated?

NEW FAMILY VACATIONS

MEET THE COW
"A farm vacation was the one time we talked to each other in the evening, and played card games on the floor, and I have a wonderful picture of Amy looking up at a cow."

Father of three.

Who's Doing the Cooking? A vacation at a place with meals and services means you won't shop or cook or clean house. Otherwise someone has to go grocery shopping, prepare meals, and clean up, unless you eat out all the time. Clarify this before you book.

How Much, How Far, How Long: Take into consideration how much time you have, how far you're willing to travel, and how long you want to spend in one place. Do you prefer to drive around or spend a week camping under the redwood trees?

Budget Realistically: Family vacation costs add up. A $2 snack for five turns into a $10 expense, and a three-course dinner for $20 costs $100 for the group. Estimate a daily budget figure for expenses, include the cost of travel and overnight stays, and add 10 percent for the unexpected. If you decide on an all-inclusive vacation, that eliminates the constant spending.

Dan took his two daughters for a week to a family lodge in the mountains, and said: "All meals, picnics, hikes, swimming, sports and evening activities were included, so it was easier for me."

Just to give you some idea of how much a vacation can cost, here's the budget of one family. The parents and three young children drove from Boston to a farm in Pennsylvania for a week, and stopped on the way home for a day's tour of a historic site.

VACATION BUDGET

Day 1. Drive 250 miles from home to farm.
Gas @ .05 a mile.	12.50
Tolls	8.50
Lunch for five	35.00
Ice cream, snacks	15.00
Sunglasses (replace lost pair)	27.50
Baseball hat	12.50

Days 2 to 8. On farm.
Rooms, breakfast, dinner one week, $230 adult x 2, $161 children x 3.	943.00
35 lunches ($8 each x 5 x 7 days)	280.00
Day river-rafting (3 people, $65 each)	195.00
Movies, gifts, toys, extras	200.00

Day 8. Drive 100 miles to historic town.
Gas @ .05 a mile	5.00
Fees for museums and show	45.00
Booklets, postcards	9.50
Lunch for five	85.00
Room in motel overnight	95.00
Dinner for five (pizza)	18.50

Day 9. Drive 150 miles home.
Gas @ .05 a mile	7.50
Breakfast for five	40.00

TOTAL — **$2,034.50**

NEW FAMILY VACATIONS 7

EXOTIC TRIPS
"We worried that our 2-year-old would get sick or be unhappy on our trip to Thailand, but she was fine, and everyone made such a fuss over her that it was a great introduction to the local people."
Parents after trip to Thailand.

Pack Slowly: It may be hard to believe but on a family trip you can't do everything the night before you leave. A list of daily tasks for the week leading up to D-Day (Departure Day) is the secret. That means you may remember to give the house key to your neighbor before you're 500 miles away, and arrange for someone to water the plants. Give everyone a bag to pack and carry. "My 4-year-old put all her toys in her daypack and took it with her everywhere," said one mother. "I didn't have to look after it."

Hang Loose: You're off! Remember - this is supposed to be fun. Promise yourself you won't say even once: "We brought you all this way, so enjoy yourselves!" Turn your reaction meter to mellow. Things may not work out exactly as you expected, but you can still have a good time.

Nancy and Phil and their two teenage sons went to a resort that offered scuba diving, snorkeling, tennis, sailing, and rock climbing. Nancy and Phil threw themselves into the different activities, but their two sons wouldn't try anything. Instead, they hung out at the pool every day - to meet girls. "On the way home, they agreed with us that it had been a great vacation," said Nancy, "and I realized we were all looking for different things."

Be Flexible: No matter how carefully you plan a vacation, the unexpected will always surprise you. The special excursion off the beaten track you're sure will be outstanding falls flat, while the impromptu stop at a corner store turns into the highlight of the day.

When Linda took her two children to see historic Williamsburg, Virginia, she had high hopes of impressing them with the charm of colonial life. "As soon as we arrived, the kids said they were tired, so we picked up some ice cream and went to our motel. We spent the rest of the day eating ice cream and watching TV. Afterwards my daughter said to me, 'Mom, that's my kind of vacation and you're my kind of Mommy.' They still talk about that great trip."

I hope this book will spark exciting new ideas for your next family vacation, and create wonderful memories to laugh about. Let me know what happens and send me any suggestions you have so I can include them in the next edition.

Happy family travels!
Evelyn Kaye

TRAVEL TIPS

Traveling with children is almost like climbing Mount Everest. You spend hours in the planning and preparation, you are under constant stress, the trip is a challenge beyond compare, you feel an enormous sense of relief and achievement when you arrive at your destination without catastrophe, and afterwards you wonder why you thought it was so difficult. Here are a few ideas to make the whole experience run a little more smoothly.

BY AIR

Traveling by plane is much easier than car travel for most family trips. Travel time is usually shorter, and the inside of a plane offers a great deal more interest and room than the inside of a car. Youngsters respond to the excitement and novelty of flying and airline personnel are trained to deal with children and can help you in a crisis. Airports offer expanses of space for running around if there's a delay and you have to wait.

When you book your ticket, you can ask for seats up front in the bulkhead, where no-one will be in front of you and there's more leg room. Remember that this means that if there's a movie, you are nose to nose with the screen. You may be able to move to a better seat if the plane isn't full, or perhaps you don't want your children to watch anyway.

The advantages of seats further back are that your children are safely hemmed in by the seats in front of them and they can use the fold-down table for their books and toys. If you ask for a window seat, they can look out at the clouds and scenery, but make sure the seats are not over the wing or you can't see much. When you're booking, consider asking for an aisle seat and a window seat and hope that the seat in the middle will be empty.

Off-peak Times

Think about flying at off-peak times, during weekdays, on Thanksgiving Day or Christmas Day, mid-day or mid-afternoon. One family with a baby always flies back early Christmas morning to her family in Minnesota. "We're in time for Christmas dinner, open presents in the evening, and the planes are never full," they said.

Safety Seats

Ask the airline for a bassinet for an infant, and bring a blanket along too. If you take a safety seat for a baby, you may be charged for a passenger seat on the plane. Also, it's a good idea to bring the seat if you're renting a car because most car rental agencies cannot guarantee one. Make sure older children know about seat belts and safety procedures.

Curbside Help

The easiest way to deal with baggage when you're traveling with children is to use the curbside service. Check all your bags when you arrive, and you'll still have plenty to carry with children. This means you don't have to wait in line at the ticket counter.

If you do have a long wait at an airport because of a delayed flight or your extra early arrival, see if the airport has a play area for children. Denver's airport has a special Kidport area with equipment and toys, as do Boston and Pittsburgh.

Boarding

Families with children are invited to board first. You may like to take advantage of this offer and get aboard early with time to settle down. On the other hand if you wait the half hour it sometimes takes until everyone else has boarded, it will shorten the time you have to sit on the plane. Whatever you prefer, always check in early to make sure you get on the flight.

Mealtimes

Generally children (and even some adults) are not particularly enthusiastic about travel food. A fruit plate or sandwich snack is often more tasty than a full meal. If you can, bring along nutritious snacks that you know your child will enjoy: apples, celery with peanut butter, crackers and cheese, apple juice, bananas, grapes, raisins. On airlines, you can request special meals in advance, but don't rely on it.

Entertainment

Whether you travel by air, bus, train, or car, take time to prepare some surprises to take along.

For younger children: pencil and paper games, short books about trips, coloring books, join-the-dots books, crayons, colored pens, cuddly toys, stick-ons, sticky tape, children's scissors, wipe-off boards.

For older children: reading books, puzzles with balls in the holes, joke books, word puzzle books, paper dolls with clothes, notebook. Tapes and music are great, or get earphones for the plane's music channel. Hand-held video games can amuse for hours.

Surprise bag: Give the first surprises in a sturdy bag into which they can put the others. Dole the surprises out slowly, say, one every hour or so. You never know how long the day will be, and it's always good to have something up your sleeve. If you have time, wrap the surprises in silver foil or colored paper.

Experience teaches that if you travel totally prepared, your children will fall asleep the moment they get on the plane, and not wake up until the plane lands on the runway on arrival. Wouldn't that be nice?

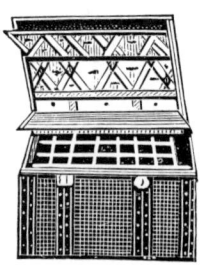

ABOUT THIS BOOK

You are reading a Travel Resource Guide, designed to provide hundreds of suggestions for family vacations from which you select the right one for your family. You'll find first hand descriptions of family vacations recommended by parents who've already tried them plus detailed information of where and how to find the best vacations for your family.

Parent-Tested Trips

The information comes from parents around the country who completed questionnaires, and were interviewed by phone or in person. People shared their favorite trips, remembered special places, gave advice on the best ages to take children along, and talked about what worked, what didn't, and what they would recommend. Also included are experiences from my own travel research and family vacations.

Every chapter presents first-hand reports of vacations by parents followed by a selection of places offering similar vacations. You can get in touch with the companies directly to book a trip or ask questions.

There's a wide variety of different ideas for you to try, perhaps vacations you've never thought of before, or things you've always wanted to try but didn't know where to start. You can choose rafting, kayaking, and canoeing, camping, hiking and biking, skiing, dude ranches, house rentals and exchanges, farm stays, free and low-cost vacations, educational programs, nature and environmental trips, in the United States and abroad.

At the end of the book you'll find resource lists with up-to-date contacts, names, addresses and phone numbers.

Who's Offering the Vacations

All the companies listed in the book provided the most up-to-date information on their family vacations, and, on request, can give you the names of people who've vacationed with them recently. Every company is listed with full name, mailing address, phone and fax number as well as a contact person when available. These companies have:
- welcomed families of all ages;
- explained any age limitations on their programs;
- supplied personal recommendations from past clients;
- answered mail and phone inquiries promptly;
- sent informative detailed materials;
- listed prices and what's included;
- a record of successful family vacation experiences.

What You Need to Know

Along with a description of trips and facilities, there's information about:

Children: Describes at what ages children are accepted, and the best age to come.

Price includes: A detailed list of what's included.

ABOUT THIS BOOK

Sample trips: Describes vacations offered with prices and length of trip, usually showing lowest and highest costs, and the range and variety of trips available.

When you call for information, check the following:

Airfare: Is the airfare included in trip prices? Some trips include it from point of departure, while others expect you to make your way to the meeting place abroad.

Accommodations: Most all-inclusive trips provide accommodations in tents, cabins, hostels, inns, or hotels, and specify if you have to pay extra for one night's lodging before or after the trip. Ask where you'll be staying so that you're prepared for a night in a hostel or a four-poster bed in a quaint inn.

Meals: Many programs provide all meals, but check if you are expected to buy the occasional lunch or dinner, and also request special dietary requirements ahead of time. On one hiking trip breakfasts and lunches were provided in the overnight cabins, but we had to bring our own food for lunches.

Materials: Ask if equipment, guides, entry fees, excursions, pre-trip information, instruction, and other extras are included, and what you're expected to bring.

The only question to answer is where would you like to go. This book can help you discover the vacation that is just right for you and your family. Browse through the pages and pick where you'd like to go and what you'd like to do. Call for information, book your trip, prepare for departure, and take off.

16 *FAMILY TRAVEL*

DOWN ON THE FARM

Have you ever felt there's so much to do on vacation that you don't have time to relax and wind down? Escape to the no-rush atmosphere of a farm out in the country. It's a wonderful change of pace. Hundreds of farms across the country welcome city visitors where, no matter how hard you try, you're liable to find yourself sitting back, going to bed early, eating well, and doing remarkably little.

WHAT'S A FARM VACATION LIKE?

City families often choose a farm vacation to show their children where milk really comes from and that vegetables don't grow on supermarket shelves. For children growing up in cities and suburbs, rushing through schedules of school, homework and after-school activities, the pace of farm life is a surprise. Every day is an adventure without a timetable: up early to see the cows being taken out to the fields, go for a hayride on a creaky old wagon, or cool off under the hose. Adults can join in, or just mellow out on the old porch swing.

For young children, it can be a real surprise to find that chickens lay eggs, and that eggs need to be collected every day. They are amazed at the sight of large cows being milked, either

18   FAMILY TRAVEL

AMISH COUNTRY

"On a trip to Amish country when our children were about 7 and 9, we stayed with a Mennonite family, in the cleanest house I have ever been in. We learned about raising chickens, which is what they did, and about the old-order Amish and how they differ from the Mennonites and what it means to shun someone and why the young Amish boys hide their cars in the fields. It's the Mennonites who host families; the Amish are too restricted."

by hand or by a complicated system of milking machines. Ducks and geese squawk on the pond, and friendly farm dogs and cats are ready to be petted and cuddled.

You may take meals with the family at a convivial round table. Some farms offer breakfast only, a real farm meal with pancakes, cornbread, juice, coffee, baked rolls, bacon and melon, and plenty of coffee or tea. At others, you'll find lunch and dinner provided too. Farm food is delicious and filling: meat, chicken, fresh vegetables and fruits, and specialties like homemade applesauce and peach pies, fresh baked bread and cranberry juice. If meals are not provided, you may have a kitchenette to prepare your meals.

At night, you'll be awed by the silence: no cars, no police sirens, no radios playing, no rumble of distant traffic, no planes overhead. During the day you're free to do as you wish. Children enjoy riding the tractor with the farm hands, feeding the goats who eat anything, riding the pony in the field, chasing the ducks. You can tour the area, visit auctions and fairs, look at local crafts, swim at the town pool, test the homemade ice cream, or rock on the porch as the sun goes down.

Be prepared to provide your own entertainment. Paula remembers that when she came back to the city after a farm vacation, friends asked what they'd done in the evening. "Well, we didn't do much. A day outside in the country air had us stretching and yawning like farmers soon after dinner. We watched some TV, we played cards, we played board games, we talked, we read books. It was very restful and relaxing, which is what vacations are supposed to be all about, but it's hard to explain that to energetic friends."

PREPARATIONS

Every farm is individual, and has a different policy for guests. Some take a few during the summer, while others can accommodate dozens of people year-round. Some invite them to be part of the family, while others treat them more like guests in a hotel. Some farms offer a swimming pool, playground and other facilities for entertainment. Others emphasize that they provide only the everyday activities of farm life.

You may stay in cozy rooms in the farm house, in a separate house, in cabins, in an apartment, or pitch your tent under the trees. You may share meals with the family or have a kitchen to make your own. How long you can stay depends on your hosts. Some accept overnight guests, others request a two-day minimum stay, and others prefer that you stay for a full week. Decide on the kind of experience you'd prefer and always ask what's available before you go.

Finding a farm vacation takes a little research. In the Resource Guide in this chapter you'll find some suggestions. State tourist offices can often provide a list of farms that take visitors. Look in your library for *Farm, Ranch and Country Vacation Guide* by Pat Dickerman, a useful guide to dozens of farms. If you are traveling in a rural area, ask about places that welcome visitors.

WITH CHILDREN

Babies, Toddlers and Youngsters

A week's stay on a farm is an ideal vacation for families with young children. Away from the city, in a family-centered community, young children revel in the easy-going pace of life, the

---

TOO FRESH MILK
"At a farm in Nova Scotia, Canada, we watched the farmer sit on a stool in the barn and milk a cow by hand, pulling the udders expertly to release a stream of white liquid into the bucket by his feet. When the bucket was half full, he invited our children to taste it. After one sip they exclaimed: "Yuk! It's warm!"
A Parent.

PERFECT PEACHES
"Our three young daughters helped the farmer's wife freeze peaches that they'd picked off the trees the day before when we stayed on a farm in Wisconsin."

NO GOODBYES
"On the last day, 6-year-old Jimmy wasn't around to say goodbye. 'He hates it when people he likes leave,' said his mother. 'It's hard for him to understand they're only visitors when he thinks they're family. He just won't say goodbye.' We understood. As we drove away from the farm, we didn't want to say goodbye either."

freedom to run around the farm without constant adult supervision, and the animals to pet. Farm families usually have children of their own, and are happy to see youngsters enjoying themselves.

Teenagers

Some teenagers revel in farm life and enjoy helping out with the daily chores: cutting hay, feeding animals, and taking on some of the adult tasks. It's an introduction to what work on a farm is like, and they relish the experience. Others may be bored by the lack of familiar activities, and miss their friends if there aren't other teenagers around.

WHAT TO ASK A FARMER

How many visitors can you take?
Where do visitors stay?
Do you provide meals?
Where do we eat?
Can we have vegetarian meals?
What animals do you have?
What do you raise on this farm?
Do you have a swimming pool or other amenities?
Do you accept children? From what age?
Are there any special facilities for children?
What is the nearest town?
What places can we visit near the farm?
What is the weather like?

RESOURCE GUIDE TO FARM VACATIONS

Bluffdale Vacation Farm
Eldred IL 62027
Phone: (217)983-2854
Contact: Bill & Lindy Hobson

Taking a ride in a horse-drawn surrey with a fringe on top is one of the activities at this resort farm with plenty of animals to pet. The daily "chore run" includes feeding the pigs and horses, bottle feeding the calf, gathering eggs, and moving the geese.

The farm covers 320 acres of rolling bluffs near the Mississippi, with winding trails to hike and explore. You can take a canoe trip down the Illinois River, go on a hayride, enjoy a cookout at Greenfield Lake with paddleboating and fishing, and sing along at the weekly campfire. Other activities include a trip to an archaeology dig, fishing, and swimming in the pool.

Every morning after breakfast you can go horse riding with trail rides for older children and riding in the corral for younger ones. The Hobsons enjoy guests. Ask to see the videotape of their farm, which captures the feeling of the place.

Price includes:
Accommodations, all meals, activities, excursions, recreation.
Sample price:
$360 adult, $240 children 9 to 13, $200 children 3 to 8, $140 under 3, one week.
Daily rate available.
Children:
All ages welcome.

Harveys' Mt. View Inn and Farm
Rochester North Hollow, RR1
Box 53
Rochester VT 05767
Phone: (802)767-4273
Contact: Madeline or Donald Harvey

For thirty years, Madeline (known as Maggie by those who love her) and Don have entertained about 20 guests at a time at their farm inn. She's written a history of the inn from 1809 when Donald Harvey's great-great-great-grandfather and his bride bought the land to the present day.

Visitors stay in a gracious farmhouse with shutters at the windows overlooking the view. Guests gather in the living room, where there's a fireplace, TV and rocking chairs. There's also a two-bedroom chalet, ideal for families with pets.

You'll find plenty to do: swim in the heated swimming pool, play lawn games, go on picnics or hayrides with marshmallow roasts, swing in the butternut tree, fish in the pond stocked with trout, feed small animals, observe the milking, and pet the calves.

The Inn is set in a green valley surrounded by mountains, with views to the south of Pico Peak and Killington. You can rent horses for trail riding, play golf nearby, and enjoy music in the park in summer. In winter, there's downhill skiing at Killington, Middlebury Snow Bowl, and Sugarbush.

Price includes:
Accommodations, two meals, activities.
Sample price:
$45 adults, $35 children 12 and under, per day at the Inn, includes 2 meals.

$450 for 4 people, 8 days, chalet rental, no meals.
Children:
All ages welcome.

"I really enjoyed the time. It was hard to say goodbye. I started crying and in fact I'm crying right now."
Claire, Lorraine, Scott.

"Thank you so very much for a very non-commercial family style vacation. The food and service were top-notch. Thank you again for the wonderful homemade birthday cake for Ryan. My lungs are just getting re-used to the smog that envelopes our daily intake."
J.L., New York.

Ingeberg Acres
**Millstone Road
PO Box 199
Valley Chapel WV 26446
Phone: (304)269-2834
Contact: John & Inge Mann**

A horse and cattle-breeding farm that covers 450 acres of rolling West Virginia countryside invites visitors to enjoy bed and breakfast accommodations. The farm overlooks its own private valley with clear, sparkling brooks, green meadows, and lush woodlands, and has a swimming pool.

You can help with the chores if you like, feeding and looking after the horses and cattle. You can stroll around the extensive flower and vegetable gardens, and orchards of fruit trees, or you can just relax on the patio.

There are dozens of trails to follow for hiking and exploring. You may find wildflowers, blackberries, raspberries, and hear the song of innumerable birds, as well as see deer, grouse, squirrel, turkey, and rabbit. Nearby lakes and streams are stocked with game fish.

Price includes:
Accommodations, breakfast.
Sample prices:
$39 adult single, $59 adult double, one night. No charge for children under 12 in same room.
Children:
All ages welcome.

GUTEN TAG!
"Dress casually because the atmosphere is informal and relaxed," says Inge who speaks German. "There are no organized activities - guests generally entertain themselves."

Inn at East Hill Farm
Troy NH 03465
Phone: (603)242-6495/(800)242-6495
Contact: Dave & Sally Adams

There's plenty to do in the summer on this vacation farm with barnyard animals to pet, eggs to collect, pigs and calves to feed, hay rides, swimming, waterskiing, and organized children's activities. There's an indoor heated pool and sauna, recreation rooms, and evening entertainment. Horseriding, lake and beach boat rides, hiking on Mt. Monadnock, tennis and fishing complete the picture.

Open year-round, the resort offers cross-country ski trails, an enclosed skating rink, and sleigh rides in the winter. Fall is the time to admire the spectacular foliage, a photographer's paradise.

You can stay in a cottage with 2 or 3 bedrooms, living room and bathroom, or in rooms in the Inn with private bath.

Price includes:
Accommodations, all meals, activities, use of boats and tennis court, whirlpool, water skiing, pony rides, table tennis, facilities.
Sample prices:
$58 adult, $40 child over 5, $20 under 5, daily rate, summer.
$147 adult, $112 children over 5, $56 under 5, one week, winter.
$174 adult, $120 child, 3 nights over holiday weekends, summer.
$406 adult, $280 child over 5, $140 under 5, one week, summer.
Children under 2 in same room with adults, no charge.
Dogs are $10 a day.
Children:
All ages welcome.

Michel Farm Vacations
Route 1
PO Box 914
Harmony MN 55939
Phone: (507)886-5392

Enjoy a vacation on one of half a dozen farms in the rolling hills and rich farmlands of Iowa and Minnesota. Near Harmony, which has a large Amish community, you can watch farmers work the fields with horses. Michel Farms is a consortium of farms that promote summer vacations in this region. Guided tours of Amish homes are available, as well as other excursions.

Take a trip to Niagara Cave, a limestone cave with unique stalagmite and stalactite formations, and a 60-foot waterfall. In Decorah there's a Norwegian-American Museum with a world-famous collection of Norwegian arts. In north east Iowa you can visit the house where Antonin Dvorak composed the *New World Symphony*. In Rochester, tour the world-famous Mayo Clinic medical museum.

Outdoors, you can go hiking, biking, trout fishing, canoeing, and deer hunting with bow and arrow or firearms. There's also cross-country skiing in winter. Among the farms welcoming guests are:

Paul and Bev Meyer, Lake City area, Minnesota.
This working dairy farm invites you to watch the modern milking operation, and just sit back and relax. It's near Lake City, home of a local hero, Ralph Samuelson, who invented water-skiing. You can rent a boat on Lake Pepin and sail or ski, drive along the Mississippi, and take the paddlewheeler *Hiawatha* on a dinner cruise down the river.

Merlin and Arlene Willford, Canton-Harmony area, Iowa.
Set in a grove of oak trees with cattle grazing nearby, you stay in a summer cottage right in the Amish neighborhood. A stream runs nearby. From the front window you can watch Amish buggies passing by or children going to school.

Erlin and Marilyn Anderson, South Harmony area, Iowa.
This modern country home welcomes visitors. Nearby is Spring Valley, where the Wilder family lived, and where there's a museum named after them. Laura Ingalls, who married Almanzo Wilder, wrote the famous children's book, "Little House on the Prairie."

Price includes:
Option A: Accommodations, breakfast and evening meal, activities.
Option B: Accommodations with kitchen facilities.
Sample price:
Option A: $230 adult, one week, 30% less for children 4 to 12.
Option B: $125 adult, one week, 30% less for children 4 to 12.
Children:
All ages welcome. Check with individual hosts.

DOWN ON THE FARM

"We invite visitors to share the 'Down Home' country lifestyle, visit with friends on a porch swing, unwind around the campfire, and enjoy fresh produce in season," says Ken Hassinger.

Mountain Dale Farm
RR 02, Box 985
McClure PA 17841
Phone: (717)658-3536
Contact: Ken & Sally Hassinger

Offering family vacations and a retreat center, the 175-acre Mountain Dale Farm in Pennsylvania lies in the scenic Middlecreek Valley with great views of mountains. This region is where Euell Gibbons, naturalist and author of *Stalking the Wild Asparagus,* lived and worked until his death in 1975.

The land is largely undeveloped and populated with friendly preservation-minded folks who know where to find the best places to pick morels and when the tender fiddlehead ferns are at their peak. A stand of huge hemlocks in a natural rock amphitheater is a monument to poet Joyce Kilmer, who wrote *Trees*.

Mountain Dale Farm has goats, chickens, roosters, ducks, kittens, horses and other animals as permanent residents. You may spot wild animals - even a bear - in the thousands of acres of state land that border the farm, a great place to hike and explore. There's horseback riding for children, and boating and fishing on the Susquehanna river nearby. Nearby you can visit historic museums, Walnut Acres natural food farm, a coal mine, Hershey Park, and Gettysburg National Military Park.

Price includes:
Accommodations. Efficiency cabins with bunk beds, bathroom, and kitchenette; rustic forest cabins with privies and picnic pavilion for camp cooking; 200-year-old log house with kitchen and bathroom; farmhouse room, shared bath; tent sites.

Sample prices:
Per night with 2-night minimum: $27 for 2, forest cabin. $60 for 4, farm house. $70 for 4, efficiency cabin. $113 for 6, log house. Meals: $16 per person per day: $3.50 breakfast, $5 lunch, $7.50 dinner. No linens provided in the cabins, but you can rent them for $3.

Children:
All ages welcome. Under 2, free. Ages 2 to12, half-price.

Olde Fogie Farm
106 Stackstown Road
Marietta PA 17547
Phone: (717)426-3992
Contact: Biz Fogie, Owner

You can visit an organic farm where Biz and Tom Fogie have farmed for about 20 years without using chemicals. They specialize in growing asparagus, have a dandy strawberry patch, raise chickens and goats, sheep, pot-bellied pigs, turkeys, and guineafowl.

The farm is set in Lancaster County's Amish country about 25 minutes drive from Hershey, Pennsylvania. Nearby are lovely places to hike or bike, antique shops, museums and parks. You can choose either bed and breakfast accommodations or one of the two efficiency apartments with kitchens.

Children and parents are welcome to help with the evening chores, which take about an hour - milk the goats, bottle feed the calves, gather the eggs including the green eggs from some of the chickens, and throw grain to the turkeys and ducks and peacocks. There's also a children's playground, and horses to ride.

"When we're all done with all this, we like to join our guests out in the screened-in gazebo, watch the sun go down, and listen to frogs croak and count our blessings!" notes Biz. "It is so relaxing to hear the creek rippling on down toward the river not far from here. The pond is peaceful too, there are a few fish in it if the ducks didn't get 'em."

"Got everything but a llama" Biz says. "I call myself a farmist, a liberated farmwife. Even got my own tractor and love to drive the baler."

Price includes:
Accommodations, breakfast, facilities. Horseriding extra.
Sample prices:
$50, with breakfast, Pig Pen Room, shared bath, one night.
$60, with breakfast, Sunny Room, one night. Babies free.
One child, $10. Other children, $5 each.
Children:
All ages welcome.

CAMPING IN THE OPEN

For many families, camping vacations are high on the list of favorite experiences. Sleeping in a tent, cooking on a camp stove, eating in the open air and relaxing round a camp fire are great escapes from city pressures.

Camping is also an affordable vacation. A site at a campground costs only a few dollars a night. In fact, if you volunteer to help for a few hours a week, you can apply for free campsites in state and national parks, as you will see in the free vacations chapter.

WHAT'S IT LIKE CAMPING?

The best advice before you take off for a full-scale camping vacation is to try a practice run over the weekend at a state park or national park near home. Do stay at least two nights because the first night of sleeping in a tent is always strange, though by the second or third night, it feels just like home.

It's easy to track down campgrounds through state offices of parks and recreation. Once again, take the time to do a little research.

FIRST TIME CAMPING
Carol and her family meant to spend their vacation at a hotel. But when they arrived, they were told their room was not available. They went to look at the campground they'd passed down the road. It was beautiful place right on the beach. "We booked a campsite for a few dollars, went out there and then and bought a tent, a stove, cooking pans, and all the stuff we thought we'd need, and we've been camping ever since."

CAR CAMPING

Zoe and Eddie took a month's camping trip in a station wagon with their 6-month-old baby. They drove one spring from Washington DC to the Gulf Coast. The station wagon had front seats that folded down, where they slept, and a portable cot in back for the baby. "We had boxes of disposable diapers, and I was nursing her so we didn't have to worry about bottles. It was a great trip and really not too difficult."

Find out what facilities the place offers. How many campsites are there? Can you book a site ahead of time? What is the best time to arrive? Is it a primitive site, which means a campsite and little more? Are there bathrooms with flush toilets and hot showers? What is the cost? How long can you stay?

It's also a good idea to check out the amenities. Do the rangers lead nature walks or present evening programs? Is there somewhere to swim or hike? Is there open space for running around? Can you take a boat out on the lake? Where is the nearest store to buy food or gas?

Because camping has become so popular, many places accept reservations for busy times like holiday weekends. If your schedule allows you to go midweek, it's more peaceful. What you'll find when you arrive depends on where you choose to go. A small state park in Delaware provided about a dozen campsites with picnic tables and stone barbecues by the lake under tall trees. At a national park in Maine, five separate campgrounds offered more than 100 campsites each, so it was an active noisy place. Every campground has its own individual style, and as you travel and camp, you'll discover which you prefer.

When it comes to pitching your tent, look for a campsite that is as level as possible, and facing south or southeast to catch the morning sun. Avoid a place near running water because it may expand to become a stream overnight. Pitch your tent close to a windbreak - shrubs, a boulder, a clump of trees - to protect you if the wind comes up.

Car Camping

If you don't like tents, you can use your car or van. It will not only carry all your equipment but you can sleep there, too. A double mattress fits in the back of most station wagons. Vans have fold-down beds and convertible sofas. Recreational vehicles and camper-vans provide everything you need including kitchens and bathrooms. Thousands of people live in RVs year-round; they move up north for the cool summers and down south to avoid winter and they know it's the best way to travel.

PREPARATIONS

Getting ready for a camping trip can be an exhausting experience. How much stuff do you need? What will it cost? If you aren't ready to invest in the cost of buying tents, sleeping bags, pads, stoves, and all the rest of the equipment, you can borrow from a friend, rent from a camping store, or camp with a group that provides everything.

Choosing the Right Equipment

Drop in at your local outdoors store and talk to the sales people. Most of them know something about camping and hiking, and will be able to show you different styles of equipment. Check out *Backpacker* magazine, which frequently evaluates camping gear; the February issue looks at what's new and available, and how much it costs.

Tents: How large a tent do you want? Will all the family share one or are the children old enough to sleep in their own tent? The weight is important if you have to carry it yourself, and you can find excellent lightweight tents. Make sure the seams are sealed and that it is absolutely waterproof. Ask for a demonstration of how to erect and take down the tent, and try doing it yourself. The process should be easy to understand, and you should be able to do it quickly. Check that there's a rainfly, that windows and doors unzip for ventilation, and get a waterproof groundsheet to put on the ground under the tent.

Sleeping bags: These vary tremendously in terms of weight, cost, and fillings. Down bags are the most expensive and when they get wet they take ages to dry out. Look for lightweight fillings that dry quickly, and bags that are machine washable. Generally it's a good idea to get a bag rated for very cold weather because you can always unzip it if it's too hot. Sleeping bags that unzip all the way around are useful because you can use them as bed covers later, and they can be zipped together to make a double bag, or used as a comforter.

Pads: Under your sleeping bag you need a pad to stop the rocks from digging into you. Once again, there are plenty of choices, but the most comfortable is some kind of air mattress. You can choose a regular air mattress and a pump to blow it up with, or an inflatable pad: you unscrew the valve and the bag automatically fills with air until you close the valve. To empty it, you undo the valve and roll it up. Another alternative is a lightweight camp bed with your sleeping bag on top so that you're off the ground.

Pillow: Experienced campers recommend taking a pillow. You can buy inflatable pillows or foam camping pillows, or bring your pillow from home. It's hard to sleep without one, and putting a backpack or folded towels under your head is never as comfortable.

Cooking stove: You'll find an array of choices. The simplest ones work on gas that you take in cylinders and attach. It's much easier to prepare a meal on a camp stove than an open fire. And don't forget the fuel.

Cooking equipment: Pots and pans from home will work in the wild, except remember there's no electricity to plug in the toaster. Plastic or unbreakable plates are preferable to glass and china at a campsite. Don't forget the can opener, cooking knife, bottle opener, and some plastic bags.

CAMPING IN THE OPEN **33**

SUMMER CAMPING GEAR
1 Bathing Suit
2 Pair Shorts
1 Pair Jeans
1 Pair Sweats
4 Shirts, long or short sleeved
2 Pair Tennis Shoes
1 Pair Sandals
2 Pair socks
1 waterproof poncho
1 warm sweater
1 warm jacket
Underwear
Hat with brim
Daypack
Insect repellent
Sunscreen
Hand lotion
Biodegradable soap
Toothpaste
Toothbrush
Comb
Towel
Water Bottle
Flashlight
Medications
Ziplock bags

Food: Plan your menus ahead of time, and fit your food buying around the menus. Campgrounds don't have supermarkets so pack what you need in freezer chests and cardboard boxes. You can pick up milk, bread and fruit along the way, and you may even catch some fresh trout. Ziplock bags of different sizes are ideal for storing spices, sugar, flour, or other essentials. Meals can be as imaginative and creative as you like. Just because you're camping you don't have to live on sandwiches. On one trip, the cook whipped up lobsters in cream sauce in a battered wok!

Gear: This depends on where you're going. Think light and think layering. A T-shirt and a flannel shirt and a sweater and a jacket are more useful than one thick sweater because you can wear them separately or together. A loose waterproof poncho is good protection against the rain and easy to pull on in a hurry. Shoes should be quick-drying and comfortable. Always pack less than you first think you need to take along. Remember it gets cold in the mountains even in the middle of summer, and there's always humidity along the seashore.

WITH CHILDREN

For some parents, the challenge of camping can be unsettling in different ways. Can you, for instance, gracefully accept an early stop at an unplanned campground because the children are tired? Will you welcome your 10-year-old reaching the top of the mountain before you do? Can you take tent-pitching advice from a teenager? And will you join in the laughter if you slip and fall into the creek on a hike? Sharing the responsibility adds a new dimension to family relationships, and though it can require major adjustments, the result are infinitely rewarding.

SLOW DOWN

Peter found family trips frustrating when his carefully planned camping itineraries were disrupted because the children wanted to stop. "I had to learn to be more flexible, to look at activities from a child's point of view, to scale down how much I thought we could accomplish. Once I accepted that, everything was fine, but it took me a while to figure it out."

Most families realize when they travel into the outdoors together that the experience puts everyone on the same level. Children quickly find out how to be self-reliant although it seems easiest to cling to their parents. Parents learn that their children are people who can be responsible when there are challenging situations to face.

Babies and Toddlers

Babies have simple needs and these don't change much when they're at home or out in the wilderness. Usually they adapt to new surroundings pretty easily if their parents are comfortable about it. Most children between 3 and 5 enjoy the freedom of camping, and the relaxed pace of outdoor life. They also like to meet new children at campsites.

A mother commented: "Our young children always enjoyed camping. Babies need food and sleep, smiles and cuddling, changing and washing, no matter where they are. For older children, camping makes them feel very grown-up, walking along the trails to the bathrooms and staying up when it was dark outside."

Youngsters

Camping with older children brings the family together in unfamiliar surroundings and changes the balance in family relationships. Unlike home, where daily routines are set and parents are usually in charge, camping is a more democratic experience. When you need someone to hold a pole while you set up the tent, your son may be much more adept than you. Collecting dead branches for a fire to keep warm is something youngsters can understand, and their contribution is really valuable. Digging up clams to cook over the stove for dinner is a

LIVING AT CAMP

Grace and her two children spent a month camping in a state park on a lake outside New York City. Her husband commuted to New York to work and spent weekdays in their two-room apartment. "It was a summer we always remember because it was the longest vacation we'd ever had. Once you get used to living in a tent, it's very comfortable, and the kids loved the freedom."

firsthand introduction to the food chain, and children can be active participants in the experience. They'll learn they can take responsibility and join in what's going on.

From 6 to about 12 is the ideal age to take children camping. They are old enough to be able to help with camp chores, they are ready for new experiences, and they like the taste of adventure that comes with outdoor life. Camping routines are easy and children can learn to unroll sleeping bags, store their belongings, clear the campsite, fetch water for cooking, peel the potatoes, stamp out the fire.

Teenagers

Most teenagers prefer to go camping with people their own age. Families who can chalk up successful camping trips with teens say that finding campgrounds where there are other families with teenagers is usually the best solution. Sometimes it's more fun to spend a weekend camping with teenagers, and then send them off to a summer camp for a couple of weeks where they can make new friends and enjoy themselves on their own.

WHEN SOMETHING GOES WRONG

Vacations are supposed to be fun. But sometimes things can go wrong. The hoped-for experience turns out to be disappointing. The weather is terrible. Someone gets hurt.

"I want to go home!"

Despite the best parental intentions, there are children who don't like the idea of animals and birds and insects and the great outdoors. No matter how enthusiastic you are, they want to quit and go home. Sometimes it takes persuasion to get them to stay. Often though, if they stick with it, they find something they like.

A friend took his 12-year-old son on an outdoors trip with another family, despite the boy's insistence that he hated walking, mountains, and camping. The father expected some tense days. But on the first evening's stroll into the canyons, the boy - an avid snake collector - spotted two snakes of a variety he had never seen before. With great excitement, he and his father stalked and photographed the creatures until the reptiles slithered into the rocks. The boy never learned to love the outdoors but he did learn to look forward to trips that would include visiting areas with unusual snakes.

It can work the other way too. Parents may have a child who loves the outdoors, but they don't. Suzanne's husband is a Boy Scout leader and experienced camper. She reluctantly agreed to join him and their two children on a week's camping trip in California. After two days, she couldn't stand it, and flew home. "I hate sleeping in a tent, I can't stand the bugs, and I'm miserable without a hot shower," she confessed, "so I let Mike take the kids. I love hearing about it afterwards, but leave me at home."

"The tent's blowing down!"

Greg and Mindy always encouraged their children to share the camping experience, but once it was more than they had planned. "We went camping when our two children were 8 and 10 with a friend's borrowed tent and our own sleeping bags and cooking equipment. We ended up on the Canadian islands off the coast of Nova Scotia. The first couple of days were lovely. The third day we drove along a rocky coast. The campground was right on a cliff overlooking the ocean waves. As we went to

CAMPING IN THE OPEN

bed, the wind began blowing, but we fell asleep. In the middle of the night, we woke up to find a howling gale shaking the tent and rain thudding down frantically.

"'The tent is going to blow down,' said our son, his voice muffled inside his sleeping bag. 'Nonsense!' said Greg. 'I put it up. Go back to sleep.' 'But the walls are blowing in,' said our daughter. The sides of the tent flapped in our faces. Suddenly there was a loud crack, the middle pole bent sharply. Greg leapt out of his sleeping bag: 'The tent's coming down! Let's get out!'

"We scrambled for our boots, jeans, raingear and bags while the wind seemed to be trying to blow the tent away. As we crawled out into the storm and pouring rain to run to the stone shelter, we saw other tents in heaps on the ground.

"Inside, campers were clustered by the stove, handing out mugs of hot chocolate. We wondered what kind of terrible experience we had inflicted on our children. The tent had blown down, we were stuck here, in the middle of a terrible storm, with nowhere else to sleep. Would this be a trauma that would haunt our children for life? Should we call off the vacation and go home?

"Just then our son came rushing up to us, holding a large cookie and saying proudly: 'See! I told you the tent was coming down! Boy, this is more fun than any other old camping trip!'"

"I got a boo-boo."

Most accidents happen in the home, as any parent knows. But they can also happen on a camping vacation. It's important to be prepared for the unexpected outdoors.

Highly recommended is taking a Red Cross First-Aid Course, which will give you a thorough knowledge of what to do in an emergency. It's especially helpful when you're away from

FIRST AID ESSENTIALS
Antiseptic
Band-aids
Bandages
Safety pins
Aspirin
Tweezers
Scissors
Cotton balls
Moleskin for blisters
Soothing cream or lotion.

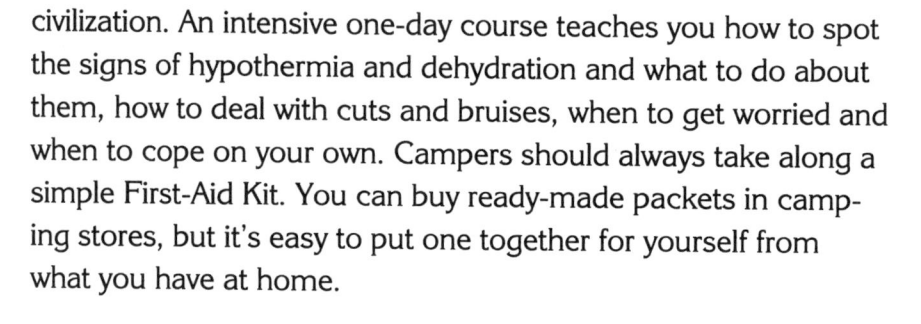

civilization. An intensive one-day course teaches you how to spot the signs of hypothermia and dehydration and what to do about them, how to deal with cuts and bruises, when to get worried and when to cope on your own. Campers should always take along a simple First-Aid Kit. You can buy ready-made packets in camping stores, but it's easy to put one together for yourself from what you have at home.

RESOURCE GUIDE TO CAMPING

Among the best places for first-time campers are state and national parks near where you live. Once you've driven off the highway and found the campground, it feels as if you're a million miles away from civilization even if you're only a few miles from home. It's a good way to find out what it feels like without flying thousands of miles away.

Everyone has favorite places: Yellowstone National Park, Rocky Mountain National Park, Yosemite National Park, Acadia National Park in Maine, Cape Cod National Seashore, the Virgin Islands National Park in the Caribbean. Think about the climate, the scenery, the travel time, what else is near the park, and where you and your family would enjoy visiting.

There are more than 16,000 campgrounds and RV parks in or near national parks, recreation areas, beaches, mountains, major tourist attractions and big cities. In state and national parks, you'll find carefully selected sites in beautiful natural areas. Park rangers frequently lead nature walks, evening programs, and guided hikes. Primitive campgrounds are completely undeveloped with only a place to camp and perhaps a picnic table. More developed places may have cookout pits, communal bathrooms with hot and cold running water, showers and flush toilets, and perhaps beach facilities and hiking trails.

Commercial campgrounds are sometimes more expensive, and may offer such facilities as a swimming pool, laundry room, convenience store, and a recreation center for youngsters.

Style of Camping: What kind of camping area do you prefer? A primitive area with only a site and nothing else? Running water? A cozy cabin in the woods with a fireplace? A well-equipped commercial campground? Backpacking to set up your own tent each night?

Pick Your Tent: Tents come in all sizes and shapes. There are family-size tents for 4, 8, or even a dozen people or small one-person tents with only enough room to crawl inside. Decide if you will be carrying your tent in a backpack, or transporting it in a car or on the back of a llama or donkey.

Choose Your Destination: You can camp near tourist attractions and famous sights, like San Francisco or Chicago. You can explore Wyoming or West Virginia, stroll through New Orleans or New Mexico. Do you long to see the ocean or walk through forests, climb hills or stay in sheltered valleys?

Select Your Climate: High and dry? Warm and moist? Warm and dry? Cool and fresh? You can find the kind of climate you're looking for by checking temperatures, rainfall and humidity before you go.

For more information: You'll find complete lists of national parks, state and local parks, and private campgrounds and RV parks in the back of the book.

40 FAMILY TRAVEL

ECO-VACATIONS

Choosing a family vacation to explore nature and learn about the environment is a wonderful way to share very special moments. Seeing elephants and tigers, or watching dolphins and whales play in the water are scenes you will never forget. Today more and more companies offer family expeditions to explore the natural world. Parents who've taken them always recommend them. While some of these trips may seem expensive, they are once-in-a-lifetime experiences not to be missed.

WHAT'S AN ECO-VACATION LIKE?

It depends where you go. Family trips to Alaska are an exciting possibility, with children as young as 6 allowed to come along. You take a drive through Chugach State Park and the dramatic Kenai Mountains, see streams where salmon spawn, visit the bush town of Talkeetna, tour Denali National park to photograph moose, caribou, and brown bears, and even try your hand at goldpanning. There's a day in Anchorage for sightseeing.

You can also spend a week learning about some of the most beautiful regions of the country. Every year the National Wildlife

"The family itinerary you planned gave my children an unforgettable opportunity to experience the jungle and wildlife of the tropics."

A parent from Texas.

Federation holds Conservation Summits in an area of outstanding natural beauty. These meetings are designed for people who want to learn more about nature and how to be environmentally responsible citizens. You'll go on field trips, hikes and excursions and enjoy evening programs.

Whale-watching

Many families recommended whale-watching excursions, available along the California coast and Eastern shores. Sandy and her family watched whales from a boat in Long Island Sound just outside New York City one summer's day. A huge whale decided to swim right across the path of the boat, directly under the bow section of the main deck, no more than five yards away from the excited passengers hanging over the sides. Everyone gazed in awe as the whale surfaced, spouted into the air, fell back into the water and disappeared.

For a different perspective, join a sea kayak trip to paddle near the whales in the warm waters of Baja California's Sea of Cortez, or explore the waters of the San Juan Islands off the Washington coast, both visiting places for whales and dolphins.

"We move closer to gaze at the closest whale, only 20 yards away. Its sleek body arches, head and tail under water, glossy back uppermost. Its ridged blowhole, looking like a giant valve, opens and whoosh! goes the spout, spray rising and spreading out like a fountain."

Parent on whale-watching trip.

Grandparent Trips

Today's grandparents are younger, more energetic, and more experienced travelers than previous generations. Several companies now offer programs for grandparents and grandchildren to explore cities and take adventure trips together.

The Olympic Park Institute in Washington has designed a five-day inter-generational program of environmental education. To qualify, grandparents have to be over 60 and grandchildren between 9 and 13. The Educational Safari takes them into the park to study tidepools of the seashore, identify flowers, butterflies, birds, mosses and mushrooms, investigate archaeological sites, find and use edible plants like nettles and sorrel, and learn how to make bat boxes and animal track casts.

Exotic Places

Joan, her husband, and their two children, aged 8 and 2, joined a Costa Rica family trip with three other adults and four children, touring in a small air-conditioned bus with a naturalist-guide and local driver.

"When we visited volcanoes and national parks, all the signs were in Spanish so it was gratifying to have our own guide. We stayed in a rainforest lodge. It was what we all imagined a jungle lodge to be, but even better. We had double rooms with screens, ceiling fans, and private baths. Each room opened onto the veranda, and from each corner of the verandah hung a double swinging hammock, just perfect for siestas."

From the lodge, they took hikes into the rainforest, mostly in the early morning and evening, and looked for wildlife. "Our guide was always there to explain. We found poison arrow frogs in neon green and electric red patterns, huge bullet ants and walking sticks, and snakes that we mistook at first for hanging vines. We saw hummingbirds, tanagers, herons and kingfishers.

"We saw communities of hanging nests of the Orapendulas, and trees full of vultures. We heard and then saw trees full of howler monkeys. We spotted iguanas high up in the trees and a crocodile in the river. At night, searching with flashlights, we picked up the large glowing eyes of a furry, long-tailed mammal called a kinkajou."

You can also join family safaris to Africa where you'll spot wildebeest, zebras and flamingoes, as well as visiting a local school to meet Tanzanian children. Other family adventures

INSPIRED

"Some children are 'into' nature and thrive on the challenge of finding creepy crawly things in the jungle. They will be enthralled. Even if your children are not so naturally inclined, they can do other things; practice Spanish, join in soccer games, learn more about volcanoes, try playing the marimba, enjoy shopping in the local markets. We came back inspired!"

A parent from Michigan.

include trips to the Canadian Rockies, trekking in Nepal, and a tour of the Amazon rainforest to explore its wonders.

Consider a family trip to the Galapagos Islands off the coast of Ecuador, which Charles Darwin visited a century ago and which inspired his theory of evolution. Starting in Quito, you spend a day sightseeing and visit the monument that marks the spot where the Equator divides the northern and southern hemispheres. You fly to the Galapagos, board a boat and spend several days visiting different islands. On the islands, you look for the unique Galapagos penguins, blue-footed boobies, giant land iguanas, and flightless cormorants. You can even swim with the sea lions in the ocean.

RESOURCE GUIDE TO ECO-VACATIONS AND NATURE TRIPS

Alaska Wildland
PO Box 389
Girdwood AK 99587
Phone: (907)783-2928/(800)334-8730
Fax: (907783-2130
Contact: Kirk Hoessle, Director

"For years we have yearned to visit and experience Alaska. Now that our dream has been realized, we know that Alaska's greatest resource is the people who display an unbounded affection for the environment, people like you. Thank you for the most fulfilling ten days we have experienced."
Couple from New York.

Since 1977, this company has been encouraging visitors to Alaska to "experience" the country firsthand with an expert guide, not just sightsee passively through the windows of a tour bus.

Guiding families on rafting, hiking, and camping expeditions introduces them to the real wilderness that many visitors miss. Your adventure may show you those unique magical moments that are not possible on other tours, such as a cow moose and newborn calf twins staring curiously from shore as you raft peacefully by.

A special Family Safari designed for active parents with children between 6 and 11 includes an assistant to look after the children's requirements. Every child receives an Alaska Fun packet of things to do during van and train travel.

Hardy travelers can join a Winter Safari where you watch the start of the Iditarod dogsled race, go on a snowshoe walk, watch the dazzling display of the Northern Lights, and photograph bald eagles at their winter gathering grounds.

Price includes:
Accommodations, meals, transportation, activities, gear, equipment, full guide service.
Sample trips:
$1,995 adult, 10 days, Winter Safari.
$2,250 adult, $1,195 children 6 to 11, 8 days, Family Safari.
$2,795 adult, 12 days, Tent and Cabin Safari.
Children:
Accepted over 6, accompanied by parents, on some trips.

Big Five Tours and Expeditions
110 Walt Whitman Road
South Huntington NY 11746
Phone: (516)424-2036/(800)445-7002
Fax: (516)424-2154
Contact: Mahen Sanghratka, President

Elephant, lion, giraffe, and other wildlife provide perfect photographs on an *Out of Africa* safari in Kenya that welcomes children under 12. Big Five is a family-owned company that has been leading tours in Africa since 1973, and specializes in taking visitors to see everything they have come to find.

The family safari includes visits to Aberdare National Park, where you'll stay at one of Kenya's famed "tree hotels," situated on stilts overlooking a floodlit waterhole. From an observation terrace you can watch nocturnal animals come to drink.

Families also enjoy an exploration of Kenya and Tanzania. There's a climb to the Ngorongoro Highlands, and a 2,000-foot descent into the crater floor, which supports a year-round population of over 30,000 animals. You may see black rhino, bull elephants, cheetah, wildebeest, zebra, hippo and buffalo, as well as thousands of flamingoes.

The company offers trips to South Africa, Rwanda, the Kenya coast, climbs of Mount Kilimanjaro, Zimbabwe, and a 19-day tour of Kenya and Egypt with a cruise on the Nile.

Price includes:
Accommodations, airfare, transportation, some tips, all meals, guides, instruction, entry fees, equipment, pre-trip orientation, welcome and farewell parties.

Sample trips:
$3,895 adult, 30% off, children under 12, 15 days, Out of Africa tour.

$4,995 adult, 30% off, children under 12, 17 days, Golden Shadows, Flying Hooves tour.

Children:
Accepted from 5. Best age: 8 and over.

Ecotour Expeditions
PO Box 1066
Cambridge, MA 02238
Phone: (617)876-5817/(800)688-1822
Fax: (617)876-3638
Contact: Mark Baker

Since 1988, Mark Baker has been organizing environmental trips mostly to the Amazon in Brazil but also to Venezuela, Ecuador, Costa Rica, and Panama. Professional scientists lead all trips and share their knowledge of the animals and plants of the rainforest areas as well as discuss the preservation of the tropical forest. You can choose an excursion or an expedition. Expeditions go a considerable distance into the wilderness and are 10-15 days longs, while excursions are generally 4-10 days long, and are available throughout the year.

One of the most popular trips is the *White Waters and Black* in the Amazon aboard a specially designed riverboat for 9 days. You will see giant buttressed trees hung with vines and orchids. Your guide will show you Caiman crocodiles along the riverbanks, their mouths open to cool themselves. On walks in the forest you will see monkeys leaping in the tree limbs. At night you can hear the chorus of hundreds of toads along the river banks.

On other trips you can walk in the high valleys of the Ecuadorian Andes, go snorkeling on coral reefs off the Pacific coast of Costa Rica, follow the trails of the conquistadores in Panama, and hike in isolated regions of Venezuela.

Price includes:
Accommodations, some meals, excursions, instruction, guides, entry fees, equipment, pre-trip orientation.

Sample trips:
$600 adult, 4 days, Amazon Riverboat Excursion.
$800 adult, 6 days, Costa Rica Rainforest.
$1,700 adult, 11 days, Amazon Riverboat Expedition.

Children:
Best age: Over 8. Welcome on all trips. The company can design private trips for families.

"Families grow to love the joy of discovery, share in the knowledge of experts in their fields, and feel the enthusiasm of group participation. The Conservation Summits help us to become proper stewards of this precious earth."
Environmental Center program coordinator.

"The day we discovered Summits was the day our eyes were opened to the world. We have encouraged many others to attend, and one of us has started to bring a new generation of Summiteers."
Two participants.

National Wildlife Federation
Conservation Summits
8925 Leesburg Pike
Vienna VA 22184-0001
Phone: (800)245-5484
Fax: (703)442-7332
Contact: Barbara Mayritsch/Sheri Sykes

The National Wildlife Federation is the nation's largest conservation organization. Founded in 1936, the Federation works to conserve natural resources and protect the environment.

More than 30,000 vacationers have participated in NWF Conservation Summits. Offered in July and August for a week in four different locations, each Summit offers about 20 different classes and field trips led by naturalists and professors who are experts in their fields of study. Topics include hikes, plant and wildlife ecology, orienteering, outdoor photography, bird-watching, geology, and environmental issues.

Educators can attend special classes on introducing children and students to nature, which cover teaching techniques and educational materials. University credit is offered.

In the evenings there are square dances, sing-alongs, slide programs, and outdoor skill sessions.

Price includes:
Accommodations and meals.
Sample weekly costs:
$560 per person, condo for 3 adults/teens, Montana.
$552.08 adult, $396.72 teen, $290 youth, White Mountains, NH
Program Fees: $250 adults, $190 children 5 to 18.
Children:
Teen Adventure Program, 13 to 17.
Junior Naturalist Program, 5 to 12.
Your Big Backyard Preschool Program, 3 to 4.
Child care is available for children too young to participate in the programs, with a ratio of one staff member for every five children, and an hourly fee of $3.

Okeanos Ocean Research Foundation
PO Box 776
Hampton Bays NY 11946
Phone: 516-728-4522

Only 100 miles east of New York City, you can take a trip on a whale-watching boat. In the summer months, the *Finback II* sails every day to look for whales. In May and June, you see more species including dolphins; in July and August you see more whales and the animals come closer to the boat. Reservations are recommended.

If you'd like to spend time in Montauk, contact the Chamber of Commerce, PO Box CC, Montauk NY 11954 (516-668-2428) which sends out a list of places to stay and information on activities.

Price range:
$25 adults, $15 for children aged 5 to 13. Discount rates available for groups.

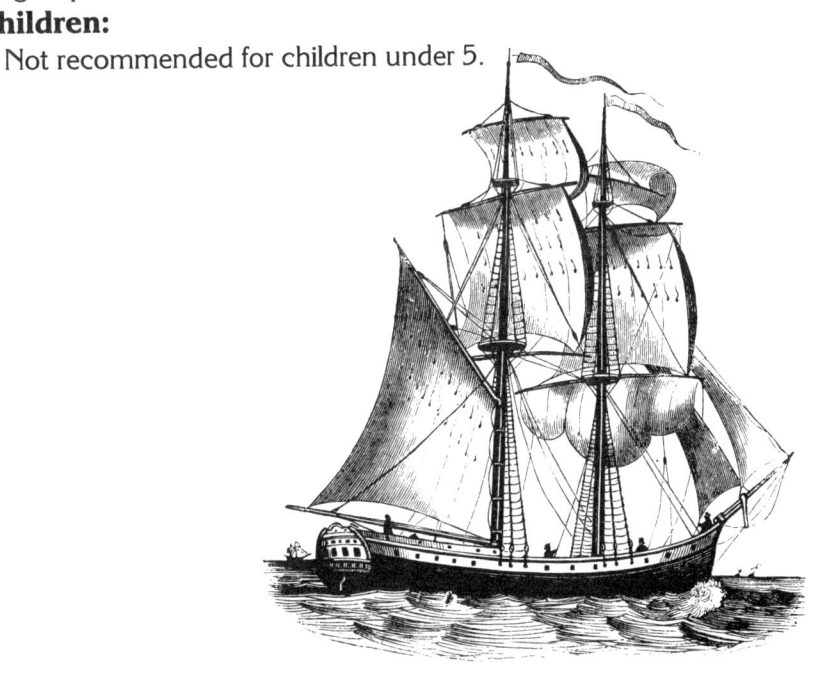

Children:
Not recommended for children under 5.

Olympic Park Institute
HC 62 Box 9T
Port Angeles WA 98362
Phone: (206)928-3720
Fax: (206)928-3046
Contact: Michael Lee, Executive Director

Olympic Park Institute, a member of the Yosemite National Institute, is a private non-profit organization whose primary role is planning and conducting environmental education courses at Rosemary Inn in the park. The inn is about a 45-minute drive west of Seattle, including the ferry ride, and is located at the foot of the Olympic Mountains, overlooking Lake Crescent.

You'll study alpine habitat, old-growth forest, hot springs, forest management, waterfalls, lowland forest, marine ecology, tidepools, and Native American culture. The emphasis is on examining the Olympic region from a natural and human perspective. Some courses are held off-campus, including trips to the Mount St. Helens region to study the volcanic eruptions.

Special courses for school groups include a role-playing game called *Discoverers and Indians,* which puts children in the role of aggressive early explorers meeting Native Americans for the first time, and experiencing the realities of trading and communication.

Price includes:
Accommodations, all meals, instruction, entry fees.
Sample programs:
$175, 2 days, Ecology of the Night.
$195, 3 days, Makah Basketry.
$220, 4 days, Marine Mammals of Puget Sound.
Children:
Best age to attend: 8 to 16. Any age accepted.

"On hikes we get to see lots of animals and it's like going on a big adventure. I've never seen a raccoon or deer tracks before."

8-year-old girl.

ECO-VACATIONS

"There is no typical day on an OAT family adventure, but there will be sports galore, fireside stories, wildlife your children have seen only in pictures, and soccer games with local children," notes a staff person.

Overseas Adventure Travel
349 Broadway
Cambridge MA 02139
Phone: (617)876-0533/(800)221-0814
Fax: (617)876-0455
Contact: Debbie Rosen

This leading adventure travel company has offered exciting trips around the world since 1978, and has been endorsed by the African Wildlife Federation because of its strong commitment to conservation. Recently, it has developed several exciting family adventures to Africa, Costa Rica, Ecuador's Galapagos Islands, and the Canadian Rockies.

Family trips with children are accompanied by experienced guides. The daily schedule is carefully planned to be stimulating but not exhausting. As well as traveling and sightseeing, you'll find a variety of experiences including learning a few words of the local language and sleeping under the stars with the distant sounds of wildlife.

Price includes:
Accommodations, all meals, services of bilingual guide and driver, park fees (except Galapagos).

Sample trips:
$1,790 adult, $1,390 children 6 to 12, 10 days, Costa Rica.

$2,390 adult, $1,590 children 12 to 17, $1,990 children 6 to 11, Galapagos Islands.

$2,190 adult, $1,390 children 12 to 17, $1,590 children 6 to 11, Serengeti Family Safari, Africa.

Children:
Ages 6 and older welcome on family trips. Call with any questions.

FAMILY TRAVEL

"We were delighted with our guide. The naturalist part of him combined beautifully with the parent in him to make our forest walks and car trips unforgettable experiences for our children. His willingness to tailor activities to the interests of the families made him an instant and continual hit with kids and adults."
Parents from California.

Wildland Adventures
3516 NE 155th Street
Seattle WA 98155
Phone: (206)365-0686/(800)345-4453
Fax: (206)363-6615
Contact: Anne Kutay

This company introduced family trips a few years ago and now takes families to Costa Rica, the Himalayas and Nepal, Turkey's Aegean Coast, Australia at Christmas, New Zealand, the Galapagos Islands, Kenya, Tanzania, Hawaii, and Southeast Alaska.

"As parents ourselves, we recognize children's needs and tailor family trips to their capabilities by slowing the pace, planning frequent impromptu activities, visiting wildlife sites with easy trails and myriad viewing opportunity, and special meals," notes director Kurt Kutay. "Guides are usually parents themselves who orient interpretations for kids and adults to enjoy."

Price includes:
Accommodations, airfare and transportation in Costa Rica, all meals, excursions, guides, instruction, entry fees, equpment, pre-trip orientation; special children's rates.

Sample trips:
$1,695 adult, 10 days, Costa Rica Family Odyssey
$2,240 adult, 9 days, Nepal Annapurna Family Trek
$2,350 adult, 16 days, New Zealand Kiwi Family

Children:
Accepted from 5. Best age: 8 to 18.

Yellowstone Institute
Yellowstone National Park
Wyoming 82190
Phone: (307)344-2294
Contact: Don Nelson, Director

Yellowstone National Park is an amazing region of snow-covered mountains, waterfalls, flower-covered fields, and steaming hot geysers. However long you spend, you won't be able to see it all. Call **Park Visitor Services, (307)344-2107**, for information and maps on camping, hiking, trails, nature programs and more.

The Institute is organized by the Yellowstone Association, a non-profit group founded in 1933 to support educational, historical, and scientific programs for the benefit of the park and its visitors. You can choose from 80 courses on astronomy, wildflowers, fly fishing, canoeing, bears, and wildlife photography, as well as programs in art, history and writing.

You can stay in the Institute's log cabins, which have no plumbing but are heated by electricity. Participants bring their own food, and cooking is done in the communal kitchen which has stoves, utensils, and refrigerators. Other accommodations are available in the park, or in hotels and motels nearby.

Price includes:
Tuition only for courses at the Institute; tuition, meals and lodging on excursions.
Sample courses:
$100, 2 days, Wolves of Yellowstone.
$330, 5 days, Canoe Trip, Lewis & Shoshone Lakes.
$299, 4 days, Llama Trek in the Tetons.
Children:
Welcome to join courses with parents.

MOONSCAPE
"At Yellowstone National Park the main attraction is the geysers. In some areas you can just walk around and come upon them. In other areas, boardwalks wind through the geyser field. When you see a large expanse of land with several geysers spewing steam into the air, it makes you think you're on the moon."

Family after week's visit to park.

Zoetic Research
Sea Quest Expeditions
PO Box 2424
Friday Harbor WA 98250
Phone: (206)378-5767
Contact: Mark Lewis, Director

These sea kayak trips are led by experienced kayakers who are biologists, and who share their comprehensive knowledge of natural history. All groups are limited to 12 participants. No previous kayaking experience is necessary, but you should be in good physical condition.

The company uses fiberglass kayaks that hold two paddlers and gear, and are extremely stable. You paddle for about four hours a day, and then camp out along the shore. If you can hike, bike or swim, you can paddle a kayak. At night, you camp on beaches, eat fresh-cooked meals including fish, salads, vegetables and fruit, and enjoy hiking, snorkeling, and fishing.

Kayakers explore the Sea of Cortez in Baja, and the San Juan Islands near Washington. Both areas are prime whale-watching centers, and promise exciting glimpses of these huge mammals.

Price includes:
Accommodations, transportation, some meals, guides, instruction, entry fees, equipment, pre-trip orientation, insurance liability.
Sample trips:
$49, one day, Washington.
$229, 3 days, Washington.
$599, 5 days, Baja California.
$699, 7 days, Baja California.
Children:
One-day trips, over 5. Other trips, over 12.

"Paddling with the whales was the climax of an entirely great trip. The guides made it seem like we were on a scientific expedition!"
Traveler from Utah.

"Outstanding! The trip went beyond my wildest expectations. The guide was extremely knowledgeable and conveyed his enthusiasm to the group."
Traveler from Washington.

NO-COST, LOW-COST VACATIONS

The world of free vacations and bargain trips awaits you if you're willing to help others. Volunteer groups offer vacations in the United States, Europe, Latin America, Africa, and Russia with dozens of groups who welcome assistance on environmental and social projects.

The great attraction of volunteer vacations is that they're free - or extremely inexpensive - and a few even pay you a stipend for your services. Some require that you bring your own food, most of them provide basic accommodations, and almost all of them expect you to pay transportation to the site and incidental personal expenses. If you are adaptable and energetic, volunteering may prove to be one of your best vacation experiences.

WHAT DO I DO FOR A FREE VACATION?

You can help with youth programs, health projects, and child care, as well as on farm projects, building and construction. Practical skills and knowledge of the language are important assets for volunteers.

"Expect to feel a bit overwhelmed at first because trail work is a unique experience for most people."
A staff person.

In The Parks

There are hundreds of opportunities for volunteer vacations in state and national parks. You choose a region, pick the kind of work that fits your abilities, and send in an application.

California: You can spend a summer in California's Redwood National Park where the Volunteers-In-Parks program (VIP) invites adults to spend a month or more helping with a variety of jobs. The park has centuries-old magnificent Coast Redwood trees from 200 to 300 feet tall, with diameters of up to 20 feet.

Vermont: Vermont's State Parks need 70 volunteers a year. Their work includes clearing trails, assisting visitors, presenting talks, and helping in the office. The main focus of the work is operating the campgrounds and day use areas.

North Carolina: The USDA Forest Service needs campground hosts and wilderness rangers. They help maintain campgrounds and trails, and improve timber stands. Indoors, there are openings for typists, educational aides, arts and crafts instructors, librarians, artists, researchers, and recreation aides. In the Southeastern Forest Experiment Station in Asheville, volunteers help organize wilderness management slide files. Students may volunteer to earn college credits through a college-approved intern program.

Maryland: The C & O Canal National Historical Park in Sharpsburg looks for volunteers year round, and gives training for those on interpretive projects and pays for travel up to 25 miles a day. You'll help with visitor services, maintenance, tree planting, and work in the museum collection.

Rebuilding Trails

Several outdoors organizations welcome volunteers to help on trailbuilding and related projects. The Sierra Club needs

NO-COST, LOW-COST VACATIONS 57

volunteers to help on its service trips in several regions, including Alaska and Hawaii. For example, you can spend a week clearing trails in the Selkirk Mountains of Idaho, stay in a camp at 6,650 feet, and enjoy the wildlife and trout-filled lakes. In West Virginia, you build a new trail in Ice Mountain Preserve and stay in a rustic lodge with swimming and hiking available on rest days. At a Pueblo site amid the Tower Ruins of Hovenweep National Monument in Colorado, you help with maintenance and reconstruction.

On The Trails: Kyle finished high school and he and his sister Barbara, 20, decided to spend a month in the summer going cross-country by bus, and spending a week in the Uinta Mountains of Utah rebuilding trails with the US Forest Service.

"We were the youngest volunteers," said Barbara. "There was a teacher, a retired business man, two college students, and us. We cut back overgrown bushes, moved fallen trees, and rebuilt a wooden bridge across a stream. We camped out in tents. The first day was hard, but once you got into the swing of things, it was fine. Most of us had never done this before. We had to learn what to do. The scenery was awesome, and we had some free time."

TRAIL ADVICE
"Progress is slow, but steady. Be prepared for several species of biting insects, to be soaked with rain, to be covered with sticky mud or tree sap, and to make friends you will not forget. Bring a willing spirit, an open mind, and a sense of humor."

Trail worker.

FIRST STEPS

To find a good place for your family to volunteer, check the Resource Guide in this chapter, and the Volunteer Directory at the end of the book. Also, the American Hiking Society's annual Directory of Volunteers is a mine of information. Some questions to ask before you volunteer:

Is the site near where you live?
Is it in an area you are planning to visit?
Is it close to relatives?
Are children welcome?
What is the weather like?
What will the work involve?
Where will you sleep?
Are there campsites or RV hookups?
Do we bring a tent and sleeping bag?
What kind of clothes are needed?
Who provides the food?
Is there a stipend?
What will the living costs be?

For national and state parks, you send an application to the director of the region where you'd like to volunteer, usually several months before you are planning to vacation. You can get forms from the agency offering the position. Make sure you provide everything that is required. You may have to supply references and official documents, which will take time to put together. Check to make sure that families are welcome. Popular areas fill quickly, and there may be dozens of applicants.

For independent trips, you usually have to join the organization and send in an application form with a fee.

WITH CHILDREN

Check with individual places on their policy. In some, families are welcome. In others, youngsters over 14 or 16 or young children accompanied by their parents are accepted. For many, you have to be over 18 to apply.

BE PREPARED

This can be a rugged experience. If you are not used to living outdoors, or spending days in physical activity, moving rocks and building bridges can be exhausting. This may be the time to start an active exercise program to get into shape. The trail sites are often a long way from towns, isolated in wilderness areas. You will learn to use the tools and equipment on the job, and to co-operate with group members, but it may be a tiring experience if you've never tried it before. Campground host positions and clerical office jobs are less physically demanding but don't offer as much time in the outdoors.

RESOURCE GUIDE TO VOLUNTEER VACATIONS

Adirondack Mountain Club
Box 687
Lake Placid NY 12946
Phone: (518)523-3441
Contact: Trails Coordinator

Established in 1922, ADK has more than 19,000 members dedicated to the enjoyment and protection of New York's wild lands. ADK offers residential lodges, camping, hiking, workshops, and volunteer projects in the Adirondack and Catskill parks.

The ADK Trails Program brings together a highly skilled professional crew and active volunteers to protect trails throughout the wild lands of New York State. The work includes hardening trails to withstand the erosion caused by the thousands of hikers who use them, improving drainage, and repairing damage. Volunteers serve for weekends, a few days, or a week or more.

Price includes:
Accommodations, food, leaders, tools, transportation, T-shirts.
Sample trips:
$40 family membership in ADK.
$15 to $20 contribution on 5-day programs for food costs.

American Friends Service Committee
1501 Cherry Street
Philadelphia PA 19102-1479
Phone: (215)241-7000

AFSC is an independent Quaker organization founded 75 years ago to provide conscientious objectors with an opportunity to help civilian victims during the 1914-1918 World War. Today, it's involved with programs of service, development, justice and peace in 22 countries and 43 program sites in the United States.

You can volunteer for summer community service projects with Mexican and other Latin American organizations. Some 50 volunteers serve with Latin Americans in small teams working and living in villages. Applicants should be 18 to 26 years old, fluent in Spanish, and have skills in construction, gardening, arts, crafts, child care, or other practical areas.

A staff member notes: "Quakers place the authority of conscience, individual religious experience and communal truth-seeking above the authority of creeds and traditions. Yet our staff and those we serve around the world are people of many different spiritual and ethnic backgrounds. We celebrate this diversity."

Price includes:

Costs and facilities vary depending on the project. There are a limited number of scholarships available.

American Hiking Society
PO Box 20160
Washington DC 20041-2160
Phone:(703)385-3252
Fax: (703)754-9008

The AHS publishes an annual directory of volunteer opportunities in state and national parks throughout the country. It includes trail projects organized by the Society. You pay a fee to register for a volunteer vacation through AHS where groups work in projects in specially selected national park areas. Good physical condition is required.

The directory lists openings in specific parks with full details of the work involved and where to apply. These include outdoor trail clearing and restoration as well as indoor services in offices, with photography and computers, and research and environmental jobs.

Price includes:
Most volunteer positions provide campsites or cabin accommodations, training, and equipment. Some offer a stipend, and a uniform.

You can sign up for a few weeks or for several months in the summer. There are also some part-time or full-time positions available year-round.

The Directory is $5.

Children:
Depends on the program.

Appalachian Mountain Club
PO Box 298
Gorham NH 03581
Phone: (603)466-2721
Contact: Trails Volunteer Director

AMC has an extensive volunteer trails program, and in 1991 over 800 volunteers contributed more than 10,000 hours of public service conservation through the program. The AMC publications on trail building are recognized as classic reference guides.

You can volunteer to work on sections of the Appalachian Trail or some of the 1,400 miles of trails in the northeast including the Catskill Preserve, White Mountains, and Mount Greylock. The group also invites participation on 10-day trail projects in parks and forests around the country.

Price includes:
Accommodations, meals, tools, first aid supplies, group cooking gear, and some equipment.
Sample trips:
$20 to $150 adult, one week, depending on program.
Children:
Most volunteers are adults. Check with the leader.

FIRST VIEW

"At the top of the ridge I caught sight of Devils Tower upthrust against the gray sky as if in the birth of time, the core of the earth had broken through its crust and the motion of the world was begun. There are things in nature that engender an awful quiet in the heart of man: Devils Tower is one of them."

N. Scott Momaday.

Devils Tower National Monument
National Park Service
Devils Tower WY 82714
Phone: (307)467-5283
Fax: (307)467-5350
Contact: Superintendent

The Tower was one of the first national monuments created by President Theodore Roosevelt in 1906. The spectacular natural rock is part of a park that today encourages visitors to follow a self-guiding trail around the Tower, with close-up views along the way.

In July 1893, two men climbed the Tower for the first first time, using a wooden ladder for the first 350 feet of the ascent. In 1895 the first woman climbed the Tower. There are now more than 80 routes to the top, and more than 1,000 people climb the Tower every year.

Around the base of the tower is park land where you may see whitetail deer, prairie dogs, and more than 90 species of birds including the mountain bluebird and the black-billed magpie.

Every summer, about a dozen volunteers work as campground hosts to assist vistors, lead hikes, and provide office assistance indoors, as well as help with the wildlife census and resource management projects.

Facilities:
Full hookup trailer sites or housing.
Payment:
$7 adult per day.

Florida Park Service
Dept. of Natural Resources
Division of Recreation & Parks
3900 Commonwealth Boulevard
Tallahassee FL 32399-1570
Phone: (904)488-8243
Fax: (904)487-3047
Contact: Park Manager

Families with children are welcome to help in more than 100 Florida State Parks in a variety of tasks. There's a free guide to the parks, which describes what different parks offer and whom to contact.

There are plenty of options: work outside clearing trails and leading hikes, help visitors as a campground assistant, present informative talks, help indoors in the office.

The parks are tremendously varied. The Homosassa Springs State Wildlife Park is home to the gentle manatee, as well as crocodiles and alligators. Boat tours are provided daily, and there's an Animal Encounters Area to see snakes and other native wildlife.

Bulow Plantation Ruins Site was once a prosperous plantation of sugar cane, cotton, rice and indigo, and was destroyed in the Second Seminole Indian War. Today visitors follow a trail to the sugar mill for a history of the plantation.

Cayo Costa State Park is on a barrier reef island and its miles of beaches, acres of pine forest, oak palm hammocks, mangrove swamps and a spectacular display of birds can be reached only by boat or the public ferry.

Facilities:
Camping and trailer hook-ups are available.
Certificates and pins are awarded for service and hours volunteered.
Children:
Welcome if accompanied by parents.

Food First
Institute for Food & Development Policy
145 Ninth Street
San Francisco CA 94103
Phone: (415)864-8555

A non-profit research and education center, founded in 1975, the Institute publishes a book, *Alternatives to the Peace Corps; a Directory of Third World and U.S. Volunteer Opportunities*, which lists openings in the US and Third World countries. Its Good Life Study Tours offers travel programs in Kerala, India, where you stay with families in a co-operative community and learn to "live lightly on the land."

Green Chimneys
Putnam Lake Road
Brewster NY 10509
Phone: (212)892-6810 Ext. 203

Green Chimneys, a farm school for emotionally disturbed children and children with learning disabilities, welcomes volunteers who assist in farm and school activities. Volunteers get free room and board and usually a small stipend.

North Carolina National Forests
Corner Post & Otis Streets
PO Box 2750
Asheville NC 28802
Phone: (704)257-4210
Contact: Human Resources Officer

The USDA Forest Service in North Carolina is responsible for different areas of National Forest covering thousands of acres of the state. They welcome volunteers to help in the Pisgah-Nantahala, the Uwharrie, and the Croatan forests.

For example, in Croatan National Forest, a volunteer with background experience in archaeology, anthropology, or history can help survey National Forest lands for prehistoric and historic sites, which may involve photo mapping and test excavation.

Their 34-page booklet details the various positions including district rangers to develop sites, campgrounds, and picnic areas; directors of evening arts and crafts programs; and environmental education assistants to work with conservation agencies and education programs. Some positions are for a couple of days a week, and others are full-time and provide lodging.

Price includes:
Accommodations, transportation, uniform, subsistence allowance (when available).
Children:
Check with park rangers.

Pocono Environmental Education Center
RD 2, Box 1010
Dingmans Ferry PA 18328
Phone: (717)828-2319
Fax: (717)828-9695
Contact: Sarah Raley

This is the largest residential center in the western hemisphere for education about the environment. Its mission is to advance environmental awareness, knowledge, and skills through education and outdoor recreation.

Located in the Delaware Gap National Recreation Area, close to New York, New Jersey and Pennsylvania with access to 200,000 acres of public lands, PEEC offers year-round programs specifically designed for families. Activities include: hiking, canoeing, cross-country skiing, field trips, and presentations on natural history.

Volunteers can help with educational programs, both indoor and outdoor, and with office responsibilities and mailings.

Price includes:
Accommodations in rustic single-room cabins that sleep up to 12 people, with a full bathroom and electricity, meals in PEEC dininghall, equipment rentals, program.

Sample price:
$79 adult, 2 nights, 6 meals.

Children:
4 years and younger receive 50% discount. No charge for one year and younger.

Redwood National Park
Volunteers-In-Parks Program
1111 Second Street
Crescent City CA 95531
Phone: (707)464-6101
Fax: (707)464-1812
Contact: Robin Galea

Adult volunteers are welcome to help in this magnificent recreation area with soaring redwood trees. They can work indoors or out, depending on their preference. Most spend a month or more as volunteers at the park.

Positions open include campground hosts who assist visitors by answering questions and providing information, naturalists to lead nature walks and give talks on the park, and clerks who deal with paperwork and phonecalls. For the energetic, there are plenty of trails to clear and outdoors maintenance projects.

The detailed application form requires two references.

Facilities:
Furnished dormitory housing and laundry services are provided.
Children:
"Family volunteering would probably not work" notes Robin Galea. Check with the park.

Sierra Club Service Trips
730 Polk Street
San Francisco CA 94109
Phone: (415)923-5522

The Sierra Club Service Trips are real vacation bargains for those on a tight budget. You get to stay in beautiful parts of the country and help restore trails.

In Big Sur, California, you clear the dense chaparral from the Black Cone Trail, and camp high above the coastline with spectacular ridge views.

In North Carolina, you improve trails and rebuild a walking bridge. In Maine, you assist waterway staff in erosion control and site restoration while traveling by canoe in this remote northern wilderness.

In Wyoming, you walk into the Bridger Wilderness to construct and repair sections of the trail. In Arizona, you camp at 7,000 feet and combine trail work with exploring Neolithic Sinagua ruins in nearby canyons.

While the work is challenging, there's always time for hikes, swimming, fishing and exploring wilderness areas. Some service trips have a doctor on staff, who donates his or her services in exchange for a waiver of the trip fee.

Price includes:
Accommodations, meals, equipment, instructions, leaders.
Sample trips:
$210 adult, one week, Arizona Trail, Arizona.
$215 adult, one week, Upper Buffalo River, Arkansas.
$320 adult, one week, Boundary Waters, Minnesota.
Children:
Check with individual trip leaders.

Vermont State Parks
Dept. of Forests, Parks & Recreation
103 South Main Street
Waterbury VT 05671-0603
Phone: (802)244-8711
Fax: (802)244-1481
Contact: Larry T. Simino

Families are welcome in the summer months to join the 70 volunteers needed to help clearing trails, assisting at campgrounds, presenting informative talks, or working indoors in the office.

The main focus of the work is in state park campgrounds and day use areas.

Facilities:
Electric and water facilities at all sites, and sewers at some.

Volunteers stay for 6 weeks. Couples work for 30 hours, and single people for 20 hours a week.

Children:
Check with individual projects.

Volunteers for Peace
International Workcamps
43 Tiffany Road
Belmont VT 05730
Phone: (802)259-2759

The annual *International Workcamp Directory*, $10 postpaid, lists over 800 opportunities for volunteering in 37 countries including Europe, Russia, Africa, Asia and the Americas. You select the program that interests you and call or write for more information. In most of them, 10 to 20 people from several countries work together on a cooperative project while they live in the community.

The range of projects includes renovating a children's home in Romania, assisting on conservation projects in Russia, gathering and repairing secondhand bicycles to be sold to support other projects in the Netherlands, restoring a medieval castle in France, and planting trees in Costa Rica.

You can also work on an organic farm in Switzerland, or provide mime and art therapy for young people with severe mental and physical disabilities in England. Other opportunities include assisting at a health care center in West Virginia or a summer workcamp for children in New York, or unloading lumber at an environmental camp in Maine.

Price includes:
Accommodations, meals, equipment, instruction.
Sample trip:
$125 adult, 2 or 3 weeks, choice of location.
Children:
Over 16 on some programs. Over 18 for most openings.

"I am convinced that we were able to become so close because we were working together for a common goal. This bound us in a way that nothing else could."
Volunteer in Ireland.

"We slept in a barn right near the horses and at night we would usually stay up around the campfire singing songs and talking. It was very hard to leave the youth farm."
Volunteer in Germany and France.

ON FOOT AND ON WHEELS

*"Afoot and light-hearted I take to the open road,
Healthy, free, the world before me,
The long brown path before me leading wherever I choose."*
                Walt Whitman.

Active families enjoy hiking and biking vacations in summer, and cross-country skiing in winter. The secret of a successful outdoors trip is to choose one that's the right level for your family's abilities and geared to the abilities of the youngest member of the family.

WHAT'S IT LIKE HIKING?

Hiking is just a fancy name for walking. A hike can be as easy as a long walk, or as gruelling as a mountainous trek in a storm. It depends on where you go.

Relaxed hiking trips take you along mostly level trails around lakes and across flower-dotted meadows with a few ups and downs. There's time to stop and admire the scenery or take photographs. Challenging hikes climb 14,000 feet up the mountains, backpack through wilderness areas, or trek along trails where you have to maneuver over rocks in unpredictable weather.

You decide the level of hiking you like and pick a hike that's just the right distance for you. You can also choose to stay at a lodge or a campsite and take day hikes out into the countryside carrying only a light daypack on your back. To explore more isolated places, you can pack a backpack with everything you need for camping and hike along routes away from civilization.

Where to Go: Parks and forests in every state offer marked hiking trails, and many parks have a map to show where the trails go and how you can reach them, with a brief description of the route and an estimate of its difficulty. Sometimes rangers lead guided trips. Ask a park ranger for advice on where to find the right trail for you and what kind of conditions you can expect. In Rocky Mountain National Park in the summer, when popular trails are crowded with hikers, rangers can suggest alternative trails through beautiful sections of the park that are virtually undiscovered.

For many families, the easiest way to start hiking is with a group led by an experienced leader, where he or she chooses hikes that fit the abilities of the members. To find a local hiking group, ask town or state recreation departments, outdoors stores, and such groups as the Scouts and YMCA.

WHAT YOU NEED FOR DAY-HIKING

Choose equipment and supplies depending on where you're planning to hike. *Backpacker* magazine is one of the best sources of up-to-date consumer information on what is available for camping and hiking. It regularly reviews a wide range of outdoor equipment and publishes a winter issue comparing quality, weight, size, and price of different brands in detail.

Shoes: Even if you forget everything else, make sure your feet are comfortable. For most warm weather hiking, I've found a sturdy pair of tennis shoes or running sneakers are ideal. They're light and flexible, and dry off quickly if they get wet when you cross a stream or get caught in a sudden downpour. Unless the

ON FOOT AND ON WHEELS 75

WHAT TO TAKE ON A DAY'S HIKE:
Water bottle.
    Always take plenty of water.
Lunch.
    Pack healthy foods to keep up your energy.
Snacks.
    GORP (Good Old Raisins and Peanuts), dried fruits, sunflower seeds, chocolate, fresh fruit, cookies.
Thermos of hot drink if it's cold, or iced juice for hot day.
Raingear.
    A poncho, or rain pants and jacket.
Pair of socks.
Warm sweater or jacket.
Gloves and warm hat (winter)
Bandanna and sunhat (summer)
Map and compass
Pencil and paper
Flashlight
First Aid kit
Matches or lighter
Swiss army knife
Moleskin
Sunscreen
Insect repellent

terrain is particularly rugged, they work beautifully. You can find lightweight hiking boots on the market that you may like to try, but after a few hours, they often feel heavy.

On some trails in rugged mountain territory with exceptional cold or snow, hiking boots with strong soles and support give you more protection. But don't spend money on heavy expensive boots unless you're sure you need them. Also, if you're planning several days of hiking, take along a pair of flip-flops, sneakers or sandals to wear after hikes.

Socks: The best protection against blisters is to wear two pairs of socks. Ideally, you'll have one pair of thin socks, perhaps made of material that wicks moisture away from your feet, and on top of that you wear a pair of thick cotton socks. Some people swear by woollen socks so try those if you prefer.

Outerwear: What you wear should be appropriate for where you are hiking. It's warm work climbing up mountains and walking along trails so think layering. If you hike in Hawaii, shorts and a T-shirt, a sunhat and a light jacket are great. If you're hiking in the White Mountains of New Hampshire in summer, long pants, T-shirt, long-sleeve shirt, sweater and even a jacket, are good with a pair of long johns and warm sweater tucked in your daypack.

Raingear: A vinyl or completely waterproof poncho is the best cover because it protects you and your daypack in a sudden downpour and allows you to keep walking easily. Rainpants and a rainjacket provide good protection, but you need something to cover your daypack to stop everything from getting soaked.

WHAT YOU NEED FOR BACKPACKING

The difference between day hikes and backpacking is that day hikers go home to bed, while backpackers carry their beds

DON'T ASK ME!
"Why is my pack always heavier going up the hill than coming down?"
                                    12-year-old hiker

with them. A backpacking trip gives you greater freedom and flexibility to explore off the beaten track away from civilization. But it means you are responsible for managing your heavy pack as you move from place to place. The great advantage of backpacking trips with a group is that equipment like tents, stoves, cooking utensils, and food can be shared, which means you don't have to carry everything.

Some backpacking trips hike to a wilderness site and set up base camp from which you can take day hikes with a light pack. Some hikes use llamas to carry the gear, so that you can hike alongside with a daypack. You can also find burro and horsepacking trips where you can let the animals carry the load.

Camping: (see chapter on *Camping In The Open*)

For hikes with overnight camping, you need a tent, sleeping bags, pads and cooking equipment as described in the chapter on camping, but with one difference. This time you have to fit everything into your backpack, and carry it on the trail with you. That means weight is of paramount importance. Look at 5-pound tents instead of 15-pound tents and consider preparing meals with one pan instead of three.

Backpacks: Once, there was just a basic style for backpacks. Today you have a back-boggling array of choices.

External frame packs have a rigid or semi-rigid frame of aluminum tubing or solid nylon. There's a suspension system or shoulder strap, sternum strap, and waist belt that connect you to the frame and distribute the load. These are the traditional backpacking workhorses, but the tall stiff frame can limit your range of motion and even throw you off balance sometimes.

Internal frame packs have flexible metal or plastic frame stays built right into the pack body. This results in a narrow structure that can be molded to your body shape, and is much more comfortable than the external packs. It's important to make sure that an internal frame pack is exactly the right size, and that it is packed carefully so contents don't poke you as you walk. However, internal frames are often three times as expensive as external frame packs.

Frameless rucksacks are smaller than the other two packs, but some can hold up to 30 lbs. These usually have foam padding in the back to protect you from what you're carrying.

Once you've chosen your style of backpack, you can select top-loading with a zip around the top, or panel loading, with a variety of zippers that open into separate spaces in the pack, or a combination of the two. Aficionados like to argue the merits of different styles, but in the end it's your personal choice. Try on several backpacks until you find one that feels comfortable for you. Always try out new equipment on short hikes close to home before you take off on a major excursion.

Watch Your Weight!

The best way to find out how heavy your backpack will be is to weigh everything you are planning to put in it. Yes, everything - your underwear, socks, sweater, water bottle, cans, tent, ground sheet, cup, fork, knife and spoon. You'd be surprised how quickly a few one-ounce little things can add up to make your pack feel like lead. Pack a very small towel, a tiny piece of soap, toothbrush, the lightest clothes you can find, and a lightweight tent, sleeping bag, pad, or you won't have much room left for your camera, notebook, or binoculars.

WITH CHILDREN

Babies and Toddlers: Even very small children can enjoy hikes. You can find well-designed child-carriers that allow you to

Linda, an experienced mountain climber, couldn't believe that her 14-year-old son could hike along trails and climb steep paths so much faster than she could. "I felt really old all of a sudden," she admitted, "and then I realized that I should feel proud that my son could do so well."

tote toddlers and let them enjoy the view from the best seat. As soon as young children can walk comfortably over uneven terrain, they can hike. Backpacking trips with young children are more demanding because you have to carry their equipment as well as your own.

Peter and Janet went hiking when their children were very young and stayed in a New Hampshire lodge owned by a hiking group. "Our 1-year-old had just started to walk, and Annie was nearly 3. The first morning, we strolled along the nature trail. It took us a couple of hours to cover about a mile with both the children walking - and stopping. Then we hiked with our son in a backpack carrier and took one of the easy trails, at a pace Annie could manage. She carried her own daypack with her lunch. When she got tired, we had a picnic on a rock overlooking the view. The way back was downhill, and we stopped whenever Annie wanted to. She felt very proud to have managed to complete a real hike. One afternoon we left both children with another family at the lodge and hiked to the top of the mountain on our own."

Youngsters and Teenagers: Older children are often excellent hikers, but inclined to get bored if the route isn't interesting. Families who like hiking find that it's the adults who get tired before the children do, and parents may find themselves challenged in unexpected ways.

Many Sierra Club welcome children. Youngsters over 8 can join a trip to Havasu Canyon in the Grand Canyon, and those over 5 can spend a week in the Lamarck and Wonder Lakes region of the Sierras, among others. Families with teenagers can take a backpacking trip in Wyoming, and toddlers are welcome on specially designed family hiking trips in Acadia National Park, Maine, and in Arches National Park, Utah.

Hiking Inn to Inn

Sylvia and Jim's two children were 11 and 13 when they took them to Vermont on a six-day hike from inn to inn. "It was a way of hiking without backpacking," said Sylvia. "We arrived the first night at a lovely old inn and had an excellent dinner. The next morning, we took our car and followed our host who drove to the end of the trail. We left the car there and he drove us to the trail head, and gave us maps and directions to the next inn.

"Every day we hiked along different parts of the Long Trail at our own pace. At mid-afternoon, we'd look for the trail out to the parking area, find the car and drive to the next inn. It was lovely to come back to a hot shower, a great meal, and a warm comfortable bed. We'd hike for about five hours a day, with stops for lunch and snacks, and it wasn't too difficult. The only disadvantage was that it was a bit boring. The trees were thick with leaves so it was like walking in a long green tunnel, and we had a lot of rain so we'd climb up a steep trail to a mountain top to find the view hidden by mist. But we talked, told jokes, played games, and it was fun to swap stories with other hikers at the inns."

Hiking Abroad

There are dozens of family hiking trips abroad. In Ecuador, a one-week trip visits tropical rainforests and colorful marketplaces by bike and on foot, with stays in charming rural inns. It's rated an easy trip without too much climbing.

Further afield, there are family treks into the dramatic mountains of Nepal. A Himalayan Family Odyssey spends a few days in Dhulikhel, offers three days overnight trekking in the mountains or day hikes from a lodge, visits the ancient city of Bhaktapur, and ends with walking tours of the Kathmandu area.

WHAT'S IT LIKE BIKING?

You can find almost as many great places to hike as you can to bike. Today's all-terrain mountain bikes enable you to travel along trails and paths that weren't possible on bikes that prefer paved surfaces. Many hiking trips now offer bike alternatives.

Among the range of family bike trips available are a camping trip in Maine, a tour of the Canadian Rockies, an exploration of Germany and Austria, and a trip through Idaho staying at inns. You can choose an inn-to-inn trip in Vermont on a bicycle and see the views from the winding roads. There are also bike trips available where you stay in lodges along the way, and national and state park trails that are now open to mountain bikes.

How Good A Biker Do I Need To Be?

Most group bike trips expect you to be able to ride for about four hours a day. If you haven't biked in a while, it's a good idea to go out on some practice rides before you a major trip to make sure you're in shape and your leg muscles are ready for the challenge of the hills. A general guide to bike trips defines four categories:

Beginners: Mostly level terrain with a few hills. About 15 to 25 miles a day.

Advanced beginner: A bit hillier and more challenging. About 15 to 25 miles a day.

Intermediate: Mix of rolling hills, climbs, steep descents, and exciting trails. 20 to 35 miles a day.

Advanced: Same terrain as Intermediate but more miles each day.

PEDAL ON!
"We biked at our own pace, in pairs, trios or solo. And whether that meant burning up the highway or slogging along like snails, it was our choice."
  Biker in California.

What Do I Need To Bring?

Organized bike group trips provide almost everything including bikes, helmets and maps. You'll travel with a support van for tired bikers and for baggage you can't fit on your bike. You'll need to bring a water bottle, camera, comfortable clothes for biking, raingear, a jacket, and a sweater or two in case it gets cool.

If you're staying at inns, bring a change of clothes and comfortable shoes for the evenings. If you're camping, you'll need a tent, sleeping bag, pad and groundsheet, and everything for a night in the outdoors, as described in the Camping chapter.

WITH CHILDREN

Most biking trips are designed for adults, or for children of 12 and over who are big enough to manage an adult bicycle. There are several trips where children are welcome. Family group trips are offered on tours in Alaska, Arizona, the Canadian Rockies, Louisiana, Montana, Wyoming, Mexico, as well as England, France, Norway, Spain, Switzerland, Hawaii and New Zealand. For teenage bike enthusiasts, there are student trips that cater to bikers from 14 to 18.

How long a biking trip you want is your choice. Pick two days or two weeks, depending on your energy and your schedule. Family bike enthusiasts might consider a tandem vacation, and share a bicycle made for two. You can find a tandem ride in California, Colorado, and France, where you stay at comfortable inns and enjoy excellent meals.

BE PREPARED

When you hike or bike into the woods or mountains, there are few basic rules of safety worth remembering.

Don't Drink The Water! Because—sadly—almost all the water in the wild is contaminated, it's far better not to drink it. You may get an unpleasant infection from streams and lakes. If you're traveling near lakes or rivers, bring along a portable water filter system, and learn how to use it. There are several models available in outdoor stores, or you can order them from outdoor catalogs. Always filter water in the wild before using it for cooking or drinking. It may look clean, but you can't be sure.

Don't Eat The Berries! Eating wild food is a skill you have to learn from experts who can tell you what's safe and what's not. Should you be traveling on your own, err on the side of safety. That red fruit may look delicious but many of the foods in the wild are poisonous. Unless you can distinguish a boysenberry from a holly berry, be cautious.

Don't Pick The Flowers! With so many more people venturing into the wilds, and exploring state and national parks, the mantra of "take only photographs, leave only footprints" becomes even more important. Indeed today it's better not to leave too many footprints, but to tread lightly on the soil and keep to the trails. In a moment of enthusiasm, you may feel tempted to pick a glowing golden wildflower or take a few leaves from a tree, but try to resist. Nature can survive if humans don't interfere. Particularly on family trips, it's important to realize that children learn from what they see. If adults treat the outdoors with respect, they will do the same.

DON'T EAT IT!

"On one trip, we found a White Angel mushroom, a startlingly white mushroom standing alone and looking delicious. Our naturalist guide explained that it's one of the most poisonous fungi in existence, but it looks deceptively edible."

Hiker in New England.

ON FOOT AND ON WHEELS 83

*"Take only photographs,
Leave only footprints,
and underwater
Leave only bubbles."*
National Park Service motto.

Learn From The Experts.

When you take a trip with an expert leader, you discover how to be environmentally responsible. You'll also be able to relax and observe the scenery while someone else looks after the details. Guided trips ensure that the leaders check that the food is prepared carefully, that the water is safe to drink, and that the campsite is not in the path of a rushing mountain stream. You can find out how to do it right, so that when your family is ready to take trips, you'll know what to do.

JOYFUL RIDING

"I liked those long days on the road where, joyfully, no attempt was made to ride as a pack. You could spend the entire day riding alone, if you so pleased, with the security of a trip leader riding 'sweep' behind."

Biker in Arizona.

RESOURCE GUIDE TO HIKING AND BIKING

Backroads
1516 5th Street
Berkeley CA 94710-1740
Phone: (510)527-1555/(800)245-3874
Fax: (510)527-1444

The Backroads company specializes in carefully planned bike vacations. Its full-color catalog describes 64 trips in 22 states and 18 countries around the world. These range from two-day tours of California Wine Country to five-day rides through Cajun Louisiana to nine-day explorations of Spain and Portugal. The company also offers walking/hiking and cross-country ski vacations.

Bikers can find several trips recommended for families including the Point Reyes, California, weekend where bikers visit redwoods, the coastline, and an educational earthquake trail along the San Andreas fault.

In the Canadian Rockies, families spend four nights in a spectacular campground where they may spot moose, elk, coyote and bear, and there's plenty of time for hiking, fishing, and swimming. In Europe, a family trip to Germany and Austria bikes through villages along the Danube river and medieval castles.

Price includes:
Accommodations, most meals, pre-trip material, maps and directions, leader services, van support, luggage transfers, tips, taxes, service charges, entry fees. The company rents and sells 21-speed bikes and mountain bikes, with helmets available free of charge.

Sample trips:
$188 adult, 2 days camping, California.
$598 adult, 6 days camping, Canadian Rockies.
$998 adult, 8 days camping, Germany/Austria.

Children:
Welcome on trips.

ON FOOT AND ON WHEELS

Country Inns Along the Trail
Churchill House Inn
RD 3, Box 3115
Brandon VT 05733
Phone: (802)247-3300
Fax: (802)247-6851
Contact: Lois Jackson

"The Inn-to-Inn is simply the best combination of hiking and vacationing we have ever experienced."
Hiker from New York.

Self-guided hiking vacations with overnights in charming country inns are organized so hikers can follow a variety of trails at their own pace and at the end of the day, find a home-cooked meal, hot shower, and comfortable bed awaiting them. The summer season runs from mid-May to October. In winter there's cross-country skiing.

Most hikes follow part of the Long Trail, classified as a wilderness trail of moderate difficulty. It follows the ridge line of the Green Mountains, and can be quite challenging. The trail passes rushing mountain streams, glacial lakes, and a variety of flowers, shrubs, and trees. There are excellent views from Mt. Horrid Cliffs, Mt. Abraham, and other high peaks on the northern section. Less strenuous woodland walks lead along back country roads parallel to the Long Trail route.

Every inn is individual. Churchill House has antique furnishings and an eclectic international menu. Blueberry Hill is a restored 1813 farmhouse with 12 guest rooms and the opportunity for a massage. Chipman Inn is a small 1828 country inn, and Mountain Meadows Lodge, a working farm for over a century, has comfortable guest rooms in the converted barn and farmhouse.

"This program is wonderful. It caters to the experienced as well as the novice hiker."
Hiker from Massachusetts.

Price includes:
Lodging, dinner, breakfast, trail lunch, car shuttle, taxes, tips. Prices vary depending on inns chosen.

Sample trips:
$62-$102 adult per night, Spring.
$62-116 adult per night, Summer.
$72-$152 adult per night, Fall foliage.

Children:
Hiking and biking programs suitable for older children who enjoy the sport. Some inns have special rates for children under 13.

Craftsbury Nordic Center
Box 31-W
Craftsbury Common VT 05827
Phone: (802)586-7767/(800)729-7751
Fax: (802)586-7768

Set high in the hills of northeastern Vermont's snow belt, close to the Canadian border and two miles north of Craftsbury Common, the Nordic Center offers more than 60 miles of continuous groomed trails skiable on a single day or week-long ski pass. An additional 40 miles of backcountry trails make this area provides a variety of wilderness skiing experience. Shuttle buses are available in nearby towns.

The Center offer classes from beginner to expert level as well as guided wilderness and nature tours. You can rent equipment including diagonal skis, boots and poles.

Accommodations are in a converted boarding school, with a variety of rooms and cottages. There's a sauna, exercise room, lounges, recreation room, and classrooms available. Excellent home-cooked meals are served in the wood-heated dining hall. Free movies, dancing, music and lectures provide the evening entertainment.

Price includes:
Accommodations, all meals, one group ski lesson, organized evening activities, and trail passes.
Sample prices:
$56 adult, $28 child 6 to12, daily rate. Under 6, free.
$110 adult, $54 child 6 to 12, Friday to Sunday. Under 6, free.
$255 adult, $125 child 6 to 12, Sunday to Friday. Under 6, free.
Children:
All ages welcome. Activities for children include skating pond, beginner ski slopes, and sliding. Instructors teach children from toddlers on up. Games, movies and other fun family events are organized most evenings. Babysitting during the day can be arranged.

Hostelling International
American Youth Hostels
733 15th Street NW #840
Washington DC 20005
Phone: (202)783-6161
Fax: (202)783-6171

American Youth Hostels recently adopted the name Hostelling International, to link it with the international organization that has some 5 million members around the world. This unique association of low-cost accommodations for travelers awards its Blue Triangle seal of approval to those hostels that meet its requirements.

There are now 6,000 hostels worldwide, including more than 200 in the US offering dormitory-style, family and couple rooms, and a range of services from laundry facilities and restaurants to ski and canoe facilities.

AYH also offers low-cost biking vacations for people who are young at heart. You bring your bike, helmet and sheet sleep sack and take off for a range of exciting trips.

You can go to the Bay of Fundy in Canada, explore the Cape Cod National Seashore, visit Pennsylvania's Lancaster County with its farms and Amish communities, travel through Massachusetts, see the Finger Lakes of upper New York state with waterfalls and forests, and cycle along the California coast from San Francisco to San Diego.

Price includes:
Accommodations, group-prepared meals, camping equipment, transportation, activities, leadership. You bring your bike. To be eligible for trips, you join AYH for $25.

Sample trips:
$655, 15 days, California Coast Express.
$670, 13 days, Massachusetts Odyssey.
$750, 15 days, French Canadian Adventure.

Children:
Welcome on Youth Trips, 15 to18; Open Trips, over 15.

FAMILY TRAVEL

"The experience of trekking in the Himalayas was more spectacular than I imagined. You came away with a feeling of awe that really couldn't be captured in a photograph."

Couple from Indiana.

Journeys
4011 Jackson Road
Ann Arbor MI 48103
Phone: (313)665-4407
Fax: (313)665-2945
Contact: Joan Weber/Lucy Dillen

Specializing in international natural history and cross-cultural tours, Journeys offers dozens of trips to Asia, Africa, South America, and Australia. All the company's trips are open to family groups in which all members are over 14. There are also special family trips for younger children, to Panama, Costa Rica, Honduras, Tanzania, New Zealand, Australia, and Nepal.

Trips to Australia and New Zealand provide the familiarity of the English language, a high standard of comfort and sanitation, and a fascinating tour of these two countries. In Australia, you explore the desert region around Ayers Rock, and Australia's high country, the Snowy Mountains, at the peak of wildflower bloom. The December trip includes Christmas festivities at a ranch.

In New Zealand, you visit nature sanctuaries on both the North and South Island by foot, vehicle and boat. You see hot springs, glaciers and mountains, and also visit the capital, Auckland, and its waterfront.

The Nepal Annapurna Family Trek emphasizes short days of hiking, great views, and special foods for youngsters at the campsites. Modified porter baskets carry children under 60 pounds if they get tired. Trips often include the children of Nepalese staff members to share the cross-cultural experience.

Price includes:
Accommodations, transportation, some meals, excursions, guides, entry fees, equipment, Kids Packs with pre-trip orientation and activities.

Sample trips:
$2,220 adult, $1,700 child, 12 days, Australia Odyssey.
$1,200 adult, $900 child, 10 days, Nepal Annapurna Family Trek.

Children:
Best age: 8 and over. Minimum age accepted: 5.

Montecito-Sequoia Nordic Ski Resort
472 Deodara Drive
Los Altos CA 94024
Phone: (415)967-8612/(800)227-9900
Sequoia Lodge: (209)565-3388

Midway between Los Angeles and San Francisco in Sequoia National Forest, this resort specializes in cross-country skiing with miles of groomed trails, two diagonal stride tracks, and a skating lane. The Baldy Ridge trail leads up to 8,211 feet with a spectacular 360-degree view at the top. There are also marked trails for those who want to explore on their own through forests and over open meadows away from the crowds, and a chance to ski among the Giant Sequoia trees towering against the sky, over 250 feet high.

You can stay in one of four comfortable lodges, or choose a rustic cabin with nearby bath houses. Meals are provided in the lodge. In the evenings there are slide shows, table tennis, and time to relax by the fire. Outdoors, you can take a night ski tour or go ice skating on the lighted skating rink.

Adult group lessons, children's programs, and guided instructional tours are offered, and private lessons are also available.

Price includes:
Accommodations, meals, snacks, orientation, free trail pass.
Sample prices:
$138 adult, $79 youth 4 to11, $20 child 2 to 3, two days, rustic cabin.

$179 adult, $118 youth 4 to11, $38 child 2 to 3, two days, lodge.

$269 adult, $194 youth 4 to11, $50 child 2 to 3, Sunday to Friday, rustic cabin.

$369 adult, $269 youth 4 to11, $95 child 2 to 3, Sunday to Friday, lodge.
Children:
All ages welcome. No programs for children under 4. Prices based on child sharing room with adults.

"A truly wonderful, exhilarating weekend. The most exciting aspect was accepting the challenge to take a backcountry tour. Due to your excellent instructors we had a wonderful time. At any age, what can top that?"

Visitor from California.

Myths and Mountains
251 Cheswold Lane
Haverford PA 19041
Phone:(215)896-7780
Fax: (215)896-9897
Contact: Antonio Neubauer or Carolyn Vail

With an emphasis on education, this company takes travelers trekking in Singapore, Borneo, Ecuador, Nepal, Costa Rica, India, Tibet, Bhutan, Thailand, and Indochina. Small personalized groups travel off the beaten track to look at the the ecological, social and political conditions of the places they visit.

The focus of the hikes is "not just to look outward at the world and try to understand it and learn from it, but also to look inward at yourself," notes Dr. Antonio Neubauer, president of the company, and an educator and writer, who leads many of the trips.

While some of the trekking is very rugged, some trips are ideal for families with children over 12. Poet and historian Maria Garces leads a trip to explore artists and mountains of Ecuador, where you will visit the homes and workshops of local crafts people as well as see the snow-capped volcanoes of the country. There's also a boat tour of the Galapagos Islands, led by local guides, where you learn about the islands straight from the "tortoise's mouth."

Other trips recommended for families are a tour of Costa Rica to see the rainforests, butterflies, and birds, and to Nepal, for an easy trekking experience.

Price includes:
Accommodations, transportation, most meals, excursions, guides, entry fees, pre-trip orientation.
Sample trips:
$2,335 adult, 9 days, Costa Rica Adventure.
$2,550 adult, 17 days, Galapagos Islands.
$3,000 adult, 22 days, Nepal.
Children:
Best age: young adult. Minimum age accepted: 12

Pacific Northwest Field Seminars
**83 South King Street
Seattle WA 98104
Phone: (206)553-2636/7958
Contact: Jean Tobin**

If you'd like to hike in the parks and forests of Washington and Oregon, you can join programs in camping, backpacking, walking, sketching, photography, or natural history with this group. It's one of 64 non-profit associations around the country that provide information programs within the National Park system.

Special programs include geology for young people in August, with a special family rate. You can go birdwatching near Mount Rainier, take a night course in star-gazing, and learn about pioneer life on the Oregon trail. Some trips include strenuous hiking while others are more relaxed.

Price includes:
Guides, instruction, sometimes the cost of van and a meal.
Sample trips:
$40 adult, Night Skies at Mount Rainier, one session.
$80 family rate, 2 adults and 2 children, Geology for Young People.
Children:
All ages welcome. Best age: over 11. Special rates for young people.

"Thanks again for sharing your knowledge of the mountain, stars and compass. I will not forget how much fun I had on my backpacking experience. You made my heart glad!"

Workshop participant

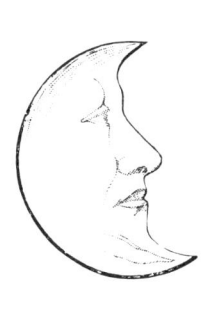

Roads Less Traveled
Biking & Hiking Adventures
PO Box 8187
Longmont CO 80501
Phone: (303)678-8750/(800)488-8483
Contact: David Clair

"Slow down to a leisurely walk or a carefree glide on a bike and explore with us the backcountry of the West," invites David Clair. He'll take you to forgotten backroads and dirt paths where there is still an unspoiled wilderness of emerald lakes, isolated ghost towns of the early pioneers, remote guest ranches, and herds of elk and deer.

It's not all biking and hiking either. Trips include soaking in natural hot springs, visiting Indian pueblos, white water rafting and horseback riding. Groups are limited to 13 people. Hiking is geared to an average adult who can walk between 6 to10 miles a day on rolling terrain and gradual climbs. Bike tours are classified beginner, athletic beginner, and intermediate. Along the way, you usually stay in comfortable inns, though some trips offer camping and mountain huts.

Bike along the Kokopelli Trail, which links Grand Junction, Colorado, to Moab, Utah, and thrill to a climb up a spine-tingling single track that clings to the canyon walls of the Colorado River followed by a 4,000-foot descent winding down through pine and aspen. Families often enjoy a Combo Trip of hiking, biking, and rafting, or the Leadville Hot Springer tour, where the route is almost entirely downhill.

Other trips hike a stretch of the Colorado Trail staying in huts, or bike and hike Bryce and Zion Canyons, designed for beginners.

Price includes:
Accommodations, all meals and snacks, guides, vehicle support, waterbottle, daypack on trip, entrance fees, information packet.
Sample trips:
$575 adult, 6 days, bike, Camping and Inn, Kokopelli Trail.
$775 adult, 6 days, hike/bike, Hut and Inn, Colorado.
$920 adult, 6 days, hike/bike/raft, Inn Tour, New Mexico.
Children:
Ideal for children over 12.

"The tour was perfect in every way. It took me about a week to come back to earth after I got home, and even now it seems hard to believe how good it was."
Traveler from Oklahoma.

Rocky Mountain Nature Association
Rocky Mountain National Park
Estes Park CO 80517
Phone: (303)586-2371 Ext.258
Contact: Nancy Wilson

More than 400 square miles of mou,ntain peaks, meadows, and alpine tundra, trout-filled streams and glacier-carved valleys make up the magnificent national park of the Rockies. Longs Peak at 14,255 feet soars in a line of jagged mountain peaks against the sky.

The Nature Association offers weekend, weeklong, and one-day classes. They're taught by experts who have spent many years exploring the region. Most seminars require hiking. The high altitude and the variable weather can make hikes a challenge, and participants should be in good health.

For a week, you explore the mountains to spot birds in aspen groves and high alpine regions with Mike Carter, director of the Colorado Bird Observatory. You can study Rocky Mountain History and visit historical sites with C. W. Buccholz, author of a history of the park. And you can go on hikes to examine grasses, sedges, mosses, lichens and ferns with Dr. Beatrice Willard, who created the seminar program in 1962. Free campsites are available. or stay in nearby lodgings.

Weekend seminars cover nature photography, watercolor painting, archaeology, mountain women, and a special Childrens Nature Program. Day trips study mountain insects, edible and useful plants, mushrooms, wildflower identification and butterflies.

Price includes:
Instruction, guides, campsite.
Sample prices:
$40 adult, 1 day, Mountain Weather and Climate.
$65 adult, 2 days, Environmental Storytelling.
$90 adult, 3 days, Alpine Nature Photography
$160 adult, 6 days, Bird Ecology.
Children:
All ages welcome. Special programs for children 4 to 7 and ages 8 and up on *Sharing Nature with Children.*

Sierra Club
**Outing Department
730 Polk Street
San Francisco CA 94109
Phone: (415)923-5522**

Sierra Club outings have expanded over the years as its membership has grown. The list in the January issue of *Sierra Magazine* now has 18 programs for families of all ages, including trips that introduce young people to the outdoors. The Club offers family trips for toddlers and older children.

Children over 7 are welcome on hiking trips with burros, where the animals carry most of the load. Most routes cover between five and ten miles a day, at high elevations. For example, there's a weeklong 30-mile burro trip from Tuolumne Meadows Campground over the 10,700-foot Vogelsang Pass, through alpine meadows, past granite lake basins and deep glacial valleys to reach Lake Tenaya.

Another travels to the Stehekin Valley in the North Cascades of Washington by ferry along the 50-mile Lake Chelan, and offers day hikes on scenic trails while staying at a ranch. And there's a 16-mile backpacking trip through the former hunting grounds of the Cherokee in North Carolina, where you'll camp in the Appalachian forest and have time for swimming, fishing and photography.

Price includes:
Accommodations, all meals, excursions, equipment, guides, instruction.

Sample trips:
$570 adult, $380 child, 7 days, Acadia Toddler Tromp.
$300 adult, $200 child, 7 days, Snowbird Wilderness Backpack, NC.
$825 adult, $550 child, 15 days, Heart of Yosemite, Sierra.

Children:
Check with trip leader for age limits.

ON FOOT AND ON WHEELS

Tandem Touring Company
3131 Endicott
Boulder CO 80303
Phone: (303)499-3178
Fax: (303)494-5826

"The company was founded on the premise that riding together is simply more fun," note owners Rod and Julie Kramer. "Clients who are new to tandeming constantly remark that they are able to share so much that they normally would have missed."

Tandem trips include staying in memorable hotels, charming country inns, and elegant bed and breakfasts as well as sharing the riding on a bicycle-made-for-two. You can bike for a week through the Colorado Rockies, or explore the Napa Valley, California's Wine Country. Abroad there's a nine-day tour of southern France ending at a Mediterranean beach, or a trip through Burgundy, renowned for its vineyards.

Price includes:
Accommodations, most meals, guides, tours. Tandems available for rental, $32 a day.

Sample trips:
$1,188 adult, 7 days, Colorado Rockies.
$2,395 adult, 9 days, Provence, France.

Children:
Welcome on trips.

"It was one of my favorite vacations of all time, and a nice way to combine exercise as well as the opportunity to stay at a wonderful bed and breakfast, taste great wine, and enjoy the camaraderie."
Biker from Indiana

96   FAMILY TRAVEL

YOUR HOUSE IS MY HOUSE

Imagine a vacation where you stay rent-free in someone else's house with all the comforts of home. How can you do it? Try a vacation home exchange, a fast-growing style of travel that is inexpensive and enjoyable. Or if you don't want to have strangers living in your home, consider renting a house or apartment instead of staying in a hotel.

The places Americans visit most frequently on exchanges are England, particularly London, and France, with Germany, Spain, and Canada very popular. In the United States, the places people most want to visit are California, Florida, New York, Colorado, Massachusetts, and Hawaii.

WHAT'S A HOUSE EXCHANGE LIKE?

The idea is very simple. Say you live in New York and want to go on vacation in the south of France. A family in the south of France wants a vacation in the United States, preferably in New York City. You swap homes for an agreed period, and live in each other's houses. The number of people using vacation home exchanges increases every year.

WHO SWAPS HOUSES?

"With very few exceptions, home exchangers are reliable people just like yourself. They are usually professional people who are interested in the same considerations and have the same things at stake. Go prepared to find something new, perhaps different or unexpected, but still exciting, at each turn of your itinerary."

*John Kimbrough,
Vacation Home Exchange
& Hospitality Guide.*

"Our exchange home in Siena, Italy, was a million-dollar apartment in an 11th-century building, one block from the town square. The host arranged for us to attend the special horse race, and would not accept payment for the expensive tickets."
Family from Illionis.

"Our home was left in immaculate condition. Our exchange partner made arrangements for us for golf times at several private clubs which otherwise would not have been accessible."
Exchanger from Ohio

Home exchanges started in the 1950s, as a way for teachers in the Netherlands and Switzerland to swap homes during summer vacations. In 1960 an American high school teacher started the Vacation Exchange Club for American teachers, and it expanded to include non-teachers. Today, there are many home exchange systems and several companies.

Vacation exchange clubs publish directories listing families wanting to swap homes. You pay a fee to join, and then receive the directories listing subscribers with homes to exchange. You contact the places that interest you and make the arrangements for the exchange. If you don't want to make the contacts yourself, you can join a full-service club, which usually charges more but does all the work of organizing the exchange for you.

It takes careful planning to arrange. Try to plan at least six to eight months ahead so you have time to make the arrangements before your trip. It's easier if you are flexible about where and when you want to go, and if you avoid peak vacation times. Most important, do you feel comfortable about strangers living in your house? People who have exchanged homes once do so again, and some people have done ten or more. Successful exchanges are made by people who are flexible, adaptable, and willing to accept new experiences even if they are unexpected, which is, after all, the essence of travel.

Advantages of Home Exchanges

Economy: You can travel more, stay longer, and go away more often if you don't have to pay for hotels or house rentals. With home exchanges, you can travel in the height of the season and still pay the same.

Convenience: Your hosts may leave you a car, information about where to eat, and neighbors who are happy to introduce

YOUR HOUSE IS MY HOUSE

DO IT!
A California engineer who's enjoyed several exchanges says: "To the prospective first-time exchanger, I say, go ahead. Take the risk. You are almost sure to like it. I travel about 30 days a year on business. On vacation, I don't need another hotel room."

you to their corner of the world. Staying in a home is very different from a hotel. You can unpack, have a cup of coffee, eat when you want to, and not worry about your valuables.

Easier with children: When you exchange a home and take children to a home with children, you find toys and games, a place to play, and children nearby for your child to make new friends. Some host families leave their babysitters too!

Freedom: You have the opportunity to do what you want without being at the mercy of a group tour. Your travel experience is unique because you live like the locals. Your host family may ask friends to invite you to dinner or show you the sights.

You can swap your primary residence or a vacation property. Typical home exchanges last for two or three weeks, though it is possible to organize shorter stays. You can also stay for a month or several months on some programs.

WHEN THINGS GO WRONG

Sometimes exchanges aren't perfect. Try to be as specific as you can about what you are looking for and what you expect before you go. One family found that the exchange home was saturated with smoke, because they hadn't requested a non-smoking residence.

In England, an American exchange family learned: "English washers and dryers are inadequate and time-consuming. You will end up at a laundromat, which fortunately they have plenty of. For a small extra fee, they will have your clothes sorted and bagged when you return."

In your agreement there are usually contingency clauses for breakages or unexpected damage, and a cleaning fee. Make sure that the agreement covers everything you are concerned about before you sign.

WHAT'S A VACATION RENTAL LIKE?

You can avoid expensive hotel bills by renting a house or apartment for a family vacation. You can find thousands of rental choices available through real estate agencies, directories and companies that specialize in vacation properties. The earlier you can decide where and when you want to rent, and how many people will be coming, the better your chance of finding good places.

Anna and Don, his mother, and their two children rented a house near the beach through a local realtor in October for their February week in Florida. "The children used to wake up early and run along the beach looking for shells. Nearby was a tiny bakery where we bought doughnuts for breakfast. We shared the cooking - my husband and son specialized in pasta and sauces, my daughter and I made casseroles and chicken. In the evenings we read books, watched TV - the winter Olympics looked really cold - and played intense games of canasta, which Grandma always won."

Renting Abroad: You can find rental houses and apartments in the Caribbean, Mexico, Europe, Central America, Scandinavia, South America, and Canada among others.

Sally, her husband and three daughters rented a villa in Jamaica in April. It had air-conditioning, pool, cook and gardener for just over half of the cost of a hotel. The family did the marketing in the open air market and Sally noted: "We bought bananas, yams, and oranges from the stands and it was a part of the real Jamaica, not what most tourists see. We found some delicious hard-dough bread in the Chinese bakery. On Friday, we went with the cook to pick out steak and stew cuts from the hanging carcasses at the butcher's store."

"Traveling to Mexico, my children never like trying strange foods, so I bring macaroni and cheese, spaghetti, peanut butter, and the kinds of food they're used to. Then I throw together dinner for them before my husband and I go out to eat at the local restaurant. They're thrilled to order dessert while we enjoy shrimp and enchiladas."

Parent of four children.

In Europe, you can find real savings by staying in a rental apartment instead of a hotel, particularly in the cities. You'll also be able to enjoy feeling part of the community.

You can rent thatched cottages in English villages, chalets in the Swiss mountains, renovated farmhouses in the south of France, elegant suites in palazzos in Venice, or a town house along the canals of Amsterdam. There's even a company that arranges tours in Europe where you stay in apartments, not hotels, and explore the area at your own pace.

"The caretaker showed us where to buy bread, milk, cereal and eggs around the corner from a supermarket owned by an Indian family. We were five minutes from the subway (or tube) so it was easy to go to the theater, the museums, the Tower of London. We even invited some American friends over for dinner one evening."

Family from New York.

RESOURCE GUIDE TO HOUSE EXCHANGES, HOMESTAYS, AND RENTALS

ASPIRE
International Friends
PO Box 1225
Brattleboro VT 05302
Phone: (802)348-7882/(800)453-6802
Fax: (802)348-7882
Contact: Nancy Mettlen

This program, sponsored by the Association to Promote Intercultural Relations, invites you to stay with local families to learn the language and understand a different culture in Argentina, Chile, Ecuador, France, Germany, Ireland, Italy, Mexico, Spain and Turkey.

"We can usually accommodate couples, a husband and wife, or parent and child, in the same host family, and place other family members with host families in the same town," notes Mettlen.

Visitors choose their dates for a homestay of one to four weeks, at any time of year. It's possible to sign up for consecutive homestay programs in different parts of the country. Visitors then share the routine daily activities of the host family, and are provided with meals and a bed.

You have to complete a detailed application form for the program, together with two references, and send a personal letter of introduction to the host family.

Price includes:
Program fee, host food allowance (where applicable).
Sample trips:
$450, Ecuador.
$600, Argentina.
$1,000 Italy.
Children:
Minimum age varies with programs. Best age: Over 15.

"Host families do not expect a boarder but rather a new friend and family member," explains Mettlen. "What all host families share in common is a sincere interest in other countries, cultures and languages. Participants are expected to have a similar interest in other cultures, and to be relaxed and courteous during the homestay."

Beds Abroad, Ltd.
188 Highwood Avenue
Tenafly NJ 07670-1130
Phone: (201)569-5245
Fax: (201)894-8652
Contact: William H. Unger

A peaceful side street facing an enclosed garden and lined with elegant Georgian mansions can be your home while you explore London. This company offers apartment rentals and a bed and breakfast hotel in attractive areas of central London.

The accommodations are close to Hyde Park, Harrods department store, and Sloane Square, an ideal location for sightseeing, and close to restaurants and cafes, as well as dry cleaners and food markets. Apartments are also available in Chesham Court near Belgrave Square, Knightsbridge, and Sloane Street.

You can choose a one-person studio, two- or three-bedroom apartments with baths, or a penthouse with three bedrooms and two baths. All have been renovated and have modern kitchens.

Price includes:
Accommodations, maid service.
Sample prices:
$76.00, double room & bath, one night/summer, Chester House Hotel.
$477.20, studio, one week/winter.
$1,444, 3 bedrooms, one week/winter, Chesham Court.
Children:
All ages welcome.

Faculty Exchange Center
952 Virginia Avenue
Lancaster PA 17603
Phone: (717)393-1130
Contact: John Joseph

Started in 1973, the program allows faculty members to swap positions in any other college without losing their salaries as long as the language of teaching is English. Areas include anthropology, sociology, business and management, computer science, economics, education, engineering, and psychology.

The Center serves as a clearinghouse for these exchanges. Each fall, it publishes a directory with the names of member instructors, their institutions, rank, and fields of specialization. It also notes the region where members prefer to teach and travel, and if they will exchange their houses.

Members match themselves with colleagues and work out the exchange, which is finalized through the department chairperson.

"We urge all registrants to initiate correspondence," notes John Joseph. "No exchanges will ever take place if everyone waits for others to write first."

FEC members have come from all parts of the United States including Guam, Hawaii, Puerto Rico and the Virgin Islands, and from Australia, Canada, Egypt, Israel, New Zealand, and Spain.

The most recent directory had almost 260 registrants representing 24 disciplines from 88 colleges and universities.

"I have successfully negotiated a faculty exchange for the academic year with a professor at the University of South Africa. Your Center was totally responsible for 'matching' us up."
Professor in Education, San Diego University.

House Exchange Program
952 Virginia Avenue
Lancaster PA 17603
Phone: (717)393-8985
Contact: John Joseph

Faculty Exchange Program has developed a House Exchange Program, at the same address. This program grew out of the faculty program, and has been extended to the general public.

Every fall, a directory of registrants who want to exchange houses is published. The most recent issue had 212 listings, 135 of them American. Each listing gives the name and address of the individual and a description of what is offered, followed by places where they would like an exchange, such as:

Costa Rica. New 3 bedrooms, 2 baths, 1000 sq. feet from beach, monkeys, coatis, many birds, peaceful, hotel/restaurants close, tropical living, all amenities, mild climate all year. Looking for Mexico, Australia, Open.

London, England. Modern 2-bedroom garden apartment opposite park, good public transportation to most of London, 15 minutes to West End. Greater Philadelphia area.

Members are encouraged to write directly to the owners of the listed properties. It's usually more effective to write to several possibilities at the same time.

Interhome
124 Little Falls Road
Fairfield NJ 07004
Phone: (201)882-6864
Fax: (201)808-1742

This Swiss-based company, in business for more than 28 years, is a leader in international vacation rentals, offering nearly 22,000 properties in 12 European countries, including Austria, France, Germany, Italy, Spain, and Switzerland.

Houses and apartments are rented on a weekly basis. The properties are rated by Interhome staff and range from simple modest accommodations (1-star) to luxury residences (5-star). They are described in full-color brochures with pictures and descriptions, with a catalog for each country available, or a complete set with costs in US dollars.

Through the company's computer reservation system, prices and availability can be checked and bookings can be instantly confirmed. US dollar rates are guaranteed at time of booking.

In France, for example, there are some 10,000 properties in all major resort regions including apartments in Paris, country homes in Brittany, terrace houses in Languedoc, villas in Provence, the Riviera, and Corsica.

In Italy, there are about 3,000 properties including bungalows on Lake Como, farm houses in Tuscany, and island getaways on Sicily, Ischia, Elba and Sardinia.

In Spain, you can find rental properties along the miles of coast as well on Ibiza, Mallorca, Menorca and the Canary Islands.

In Switzerland, rentals are available in all major ski areas, and in centrally located Lucerne, from which day trips can be taken by car or rail.

In Germany, there are rentals in holiday villages with swimming pools, miniature golf courses and special programs for families.

Intervac US
International Home Exchange
PO Box 190070
San Francisco CA 94119
Phone: (415)435-3497
Fax: (415)386-6853

Intervac International began in 1953, and today has some 8,000 listings. More than 80 percent of the listings are outside the United States with the majority in France, followed by England, Sweden, Denmark, the Netherlands, Spain, Switzerland and Germany.

There are also listings in Iceland, India, Luxembourg, Hong Kong, Portugal, and Zimbabwe. The membership is mostly upscale, professional and in education. A directory is published every year in February with supplements in April and June.

The Intervac International Affiliates in 26 countries invite individuals to join local groups, which, in the United States, is in San Francisco.

The Central Office address is:
Intervac International
Box 12066
S 19112 Kristianstad
Sweden

FAMILY TRAVEL

Untours Idyll Ltd.
PO Box 405
Media PA 19063
Phone: (215)565-5242
Fax: (215)565-5142
Contact: Harold E. Taussig, President

Idyll Ltd has created an unusual vacation mix. Created 18 years ago, it blends European package tours with the freedom of individual travel. Idyll arranges the air transportation and an apartment in the city of your choice. After a guide gives you an introduction to the area, you are free to explore on your own as a traveler, not a tourist.

The concept was created by Dr. Harold E. Taussig, an educator, author, and ex-cattle rancher. He led the first tour to Switzerland with six clients in 1975. Today, more than 20,000 people have traveled with the company, and many have been on five or more Untours. Destinations include Austria, France, Germany, Switzerland, Vienna, Budapest and Prague.

Your three-week tour of Vienna, Budapest, and Prague flies you to Vienna and takes you to your own apartment with a separate entrance, bathroom, kitchen, bedroom and living room. Linens and taxes are included. On your first day, an Idyll representative gives you an introduction to the city and then you can explore it at your own pace.

After a week, you travel to Budapest by train to find your next apartment in the castled hills of Buda overlooking a section of the Danube river. There's a guided tour of the city, and you're on your own. The third week you travel to Prague to your apartment, are given an orientation by a representative, and tour Czechoslovakia while you stay in the fascinating medieval castle district of the city.

For many people this is an ideal way to travel. A couple from Florida commented: "This is the way to go! All arrangements made in advance by Idyll. We had a home base to travel from and return to. No packing up and moving every day. We did not have to be at any place at any particular time. We arranged our schedule from day to day according to whim and weather. No pressures."

"Really enjoyed the way the whole program worked. We can honestly say it was one of our best vacations, and we go a lot!"
A California couple.

FIRST TIME ABROAD!
"We were a little nervous on our first trip abroad. Because of your excellent books and information, plus the reception in Zurich, all of our fears were quickly alleviated. We felt like we belonged to a big family."
Family from Arizona in Switzerland.

Vacation Exchange Club
PO Box 820
Haleiwa HI 96712
Phone: (808)638-8747/(800)638-3841
Fax: (808)638-5184
Contact: Karl and Debby Costabel

The largest single exchange agency in the world, VEC has about 2,000 listings in the United States, part of the Directory Group Association directory with more than 6,000 listings in 50 countries. VEC publishes directories in February and April, and the information is updated to members through computer networks including CompuServe, MCI Mail, and Internet.

The directories not only list home exchanges but include bed and breakfasts, rentals, travel companions, house-sitting, and informal social exchanges.

California has the most listings with Florida, New York State, and Massachusetts next, and Hawaii and Colorado popular too.

Abroad, England has the most foreign listings, particularly the London area, followed by Germany, Belgium, the Netherlands, France, Spain, and Italy. There are also listings for more exotic locales including Guadeloupe, Thailand, the Virgin Islands, Morocco and Senegal.

Most members are upscale, professional people with about a quarter of them in teaching and education.

Villas and Apartments Abroad Ltd.
420 Madison Avenue
New York NY 10017
Phone: (212)759--1025
Fax: (212)755-8316
Contact: Sylvia Delvaille Jones

This company specializes in rental villas and apartments in Jamaica, the Caribbean, Mexico, Italy, France, England, and other European countries. Most of them are upscale and elegantly appointed. Rates in summer are lower than those in winter.

110   FAMILY TRAVEL

OVER THE SEAS AND FAR AWAY

"For my part, I travel not to go anywhere, but to go. I travel for travel's sake. The great affair is to move."
— R. L. Stevenson.

Traveling abroad is an adventure. The excitement of exotic foods, the delights of new sights and smells, the fascination of different cultures are part of the pleasures of foreign travel. But when you travel with children, the perspective changes. Two-year-olds miss their favorite blanket, 8-year-olds don't want to try icky foods, and 13-year-olds prefer TV to museums.

Many parents are reluctant to take children abroad. Today, there are new ways to make the experience a positive one. You can travel with group tours designed for families, stay with families abroad and live like the locals do, stay in informal lodges and hotels, or take a skiing vacation.

WHAT'S A VACATION ABROAD LIKE?

Katie, 14, Donna, 12, their parents and grandmother went to the Netherlands for their first trip abroad. They traveled with a group of five parents, 16 grandparents, and 19 children on FamilyHostel, a new vacation program for families organized by the University of New Hampshire.

"Our aim is to provide a chance for families to explore international cultures and to learn together," explained Robert

McCaffery, developer and manager of the program, who went along with his wife and two children, aged 9 and 11.

The families stayed at a conference center in a village near Amsterdam. Every day there were excursions: to a Dutch school, a cheese factory, the Van Gogh Museum, the parliament buildings, and a 17th-century castle. In the evenings, they attended talks and watched videos about Dutch history and art, and met with some of the Dutch families in the area. There was time for picnics and hikes into the countryside, too.

Katie described the trip as "awesome," and particularly liked the Anne Frank House and the boat tour of the Amsterdam canals. Her father enjoyed the informative talks about the places visited. Her mother most enjoyed spending an evening with a Dutch family. "The people were open and welcoming, and we made lasting friends," she said. Katie's grandmother felt: "Our shared concerns for the young people was evident."

Traveling On Your Own

Many families enjoy discovering Europe on their own. Lil, her husband and their three school-age children spent a month traveling through Denmark, France, Switzerland, and Italy. Their system was simple: "We had no plans, only Eurailpasses so we could take the train anywhere. The spontaneity made it a trip of adventure and surprises. We ended up visiting the birthplace of my husband's parents on an island in the Bay of Naples. It was also an advantage traveling with young children because it meant that we met all kinds of people along the way. What's interesting is now the children are older, they still talk about the trip."

Carol and her husband rented a car to drive through France and Italy with their two teenage sons for three weeks one summer. They planned the route carefully because, as Carol ex-

> "Travelling is the ruin of all happiness. There's no looking at a building after seeing Italy."
> *Fanny Burney.*

> "For two weeks, we lived as the French do. We wept when we left and have invitations to return at any time."
> *Couple from Idaho.*

plained: "I wanted to show the boys some of the highlights of France and Italy. I remember especially seeing our 17-year-old's eyes after winding through narrow streets and coming up in the Piazza San Marco in Venice. Even the most sophisticated teenager is in awe! It's a wonderful idea to introduce children to Europe, so when they go back on their own, they have an idea of what they would like to see again."

Family stays: For an intimate perspective of life abroad, you can arrange to stay with a family to learn the language and appreciate the culture. Homestay programs offer this opportunity in France, Germany, Vietnam, Argentina, Chile, Ecuador, Jamaica, or Polynesia among dozens of choices. One couple arranged to spend a week with two families in France and found:

"Both families were warm and hospitable, offering us comfortable accommodations and delicious meals. They treated us immediately as members of the family, introduced us to their friends, neighbors and other family members, entertained for us and accompanied us on many sightseeing trips. We felt completely at home in both settings, helping with household chores, marketing, fetching the children from school."

Kibbutz hotels: In the Middle East, Israel offers a variety of travel experiences for family travelers. A refreshing place to visit is a kibbutz hotel designed for vacations. You'll find swimming pools, hiking trails, and excursions in an informal communal setting. There's even a dude ranch in the Galilean hills, run by a Chicago couple.

Soviet stay: A new tourism venture in Russia offers bed-and-breakfast homes to learn what life is like for average people under the new regime where many families lack modern bathrooms, safe drinking water, or enough food.

RESOURCE GUIDE TO OVERSEAS VACATIONS

American Institute for Foreign Study
102 Greenwich Avenue
Greenwich CT 06830
Phone: (203)869-9090/(800)727-2437
Fax: (203)869-9615
Contact: College Division

For travelers who'd like to focus on an academic subject abroad, AIFS has a wide range of options for you to choose from.

This nation-wide organization offers overseas study and travel programs for students of all ages. More than 350,000 students have enrolled in AIFS programs in Europe, Africa, Australia and Asia since 1964. Membership in the Institute is open to anyone interested in study abroad.

The free annual College Catalog gives complete details of courses available, together with academic requirements, summer programs, campus, travel information, photos and maps.

You can spend a few weeks or several months in the summer studying in Australia, Britain, China, Italy, or spend several months abroad through the Academic Year Abroad programs. Courses abroad cover movies, indigenous peoples, art history, and contemporary life as well as language and literature.

Price includes:
Accommodations, some meals, tuition.
Sample trips:
$3,949 including airfare for summer at university, Australia.
$6,695, three months, University of Paris, France.
Children:
18 and over for most programs.

Avenir Adventures
1790 Bonanza Drive/Suite 230
PO Box 2730
Park City UT 84060
Phone: (801)649-2495/(800)367-3230
Contact: Shirley Smith

Described as "innovative journeys for the spirited traveler," these overseas adventure tours offer year-round hiking, touring, rafting, cruising, and skiing tours in China, Turkey, France, Greece, and India. Trips are graded by difficulty, with easy walking and sightseeing on some, more active hiking or skiing on others, and challenging hikes in high elevations and advanced skiing programs on the most difficult.

In Turkey, you visit the bazaars of Istanbul, see the whirling dervishes of Konya, and cruise the Aegean coast on a private yacht. In China, the emphasis is on ancient and contemporary Chinese culture with tours from Beijing to the ethnic regions of the southwest. In France, there's a ski tour adventure in the French Alps, where you ski on backcountry runs and stay in mountain lodges.

Price includes:
Accommodations, transportation, meals, activities, entrance fees, lift passes, guides.
Sample trips:
$1,250 adult, 7 days, Ski Safari, France.
$2,595 adult, 16 days, Ottoman Odyssey, Greece and Turkey.
$3,895 adult, 22 days, The Arts of China.
Children:
Over 14 accepted on all trips. Ask about family trips.

FamilyHostel
University of New Hampshire
6 Garrison Avenue
Durham NH 03824
Phone: (603)862-1147/(800)733-9753
Fax: (603)862-1113
Contact: Robert P. McCaffery

FamilyHostel, which began in 1991, offers 10-day excursions for families to the Netherlands, Prague, Spain, Switzerland, and Mexico, with the emphasis on cultural events and learning about the countries visited. The program is modeled after the university's Interhostel program for travelers 50 and older.

In Mexico, you spend a week in Cuernavaca, the city of eternal spring, and three days in Mexico City. You visit village markets, the colonial town of Taxco set on steep cobbled streets, and the Pre-Columbian site of Tepozteca.

In Czechoslovakia, you stay in Smilovice by a lake in the Vitava River Valley, and meet a group of Czech families who are studying English there. You tour Prague and visit Hradcany Castle, St. Vitas Cathedral, the National Museum, and attend a performance at the opera or the National Puppet Theater.

In Leysin, Switzerland, you take a boat ride to Lausanne, a trip up a mountain to learn about alpine ecology, and visit Geneva, with tours of the United Nations, International Red Cross, and the Old City.

Price includes:
Airfare, accommodations, meals, presentations, field trips, social and cultural activities.

Sample trips:
$1,495 adult, $1,395 child 12 to 15, $1,295 child 8 to 11, Mexico.

$2,085 adult, $1,855 child 12 to 15, $1,795 child 8 to 11, Netherlands.

$2,395 adult, $2,310 child 12 to 15, $2,290 child 8 to 11, Switzerland.

Children:
Accepted from age 6. Best age: 8 to 14.

"Children, grandparents and parents will learn about the place they're visiting, and about each other. Sharing a common experience will provide memories for a lifetime"
Robert McCaffery.

Forum Travel International
91 Gregory Lane/Suite 21
Pleasant Hill CA 94523
Phone: (510)671-2900
Fax:(510)671-2993

Founded in 1965, this company has developed dozens of unique travel programs that focus on nature, wildlife, river-rafting, windsurfing, spelunking, fishing and bird-watching.

Several family trips visit South America. In Venezuela, you can see Angel Falls, the world's highest falls, more than twice the height of New York's Empire State building. You can trek in the world's last real jungle of Las Nieves, 300 miles south of the capital of Caracas, and stay in a lodge built according to local construction techniques with straw roofs. You can laze on a coral island in Los Roques, to swim, snorkel, scuba and fish in pristine Caribbean waters.

Other trips tour Costa Rica, visit the natural world of Mexico, explore Belize, and go to Paraguay and Brazil. There's a cruise to Antarctica, with the Russian Society for Polar Exploration, and a trip to Australia's Heron Island on the Great Barrier Reef. You can visit Austria, France, Germany, and Ireland where you cycle along peaceful country roads and stay in friendly guest houses.

Price includes:
Airfare, accommodations, breakfast, transportation, gear, equipment, map, tour guide.

Sample trips:
$525 adult, 8 days, Ireland Cycling Safari (no airfare included).
$974 adult, 8 days, Costa Rica Adventure.
$2,995 adult, Antarctic cruise.

Children:
All ages welcome, depending on trip.

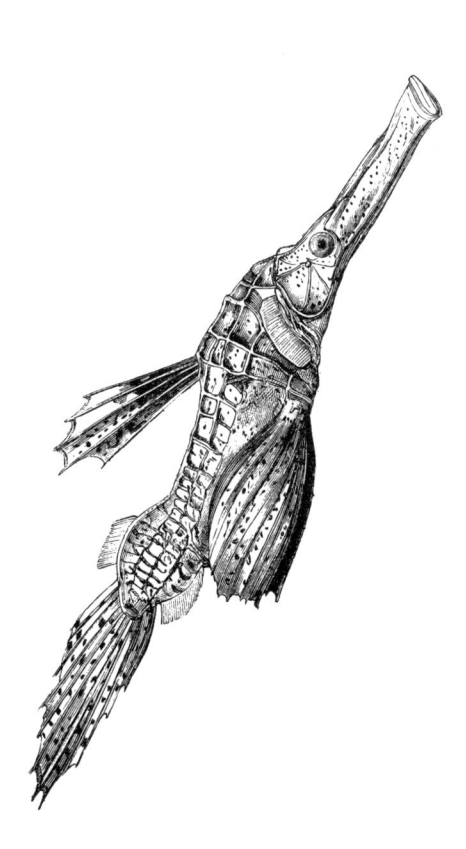

FAMILY TRAVEL

"A hotel is a place where you sleep. Here, I am at home."

Kibbutz guest.

Israel Kibbutz Hotels
20 South Van Brunt Street
Englewood NJ 07631
Phone: (201)816-0830
Fax: (201)816-0633

A kibbutz is a collective farm settlement, based on cooperative principles. The first one was established in 1909, and today there are about 250 settlements and 100,000 members - 4 percent of the population - scattered around the country.

Kibbutzim have always welcomed guests, and in the early days, guests paid nothing but helped with the work. Today, guests can stay in 26 Kibbutz Hotels, pay reasonable rates, and enjoy a range of facilities from individual bungalows to large hotel complexes. Most rooms are air-conditioned and have private baths. Guests usually live apart from kibbutz members, learn about communal life through lectures and slide presentations, and are taken on guided tours.

Nof Ginosaur, a motel-like complex with simply furnished rooms, is magnificently situated on the western shore of the Sea of Galilee, and you can rent kayaks, sailboats, and windsurfers at a private beach.

Kibbutz Nachsholim, popular with Israeli families, is situated on one of Israel's loveliest beaches, where you stay in beach cottages for up to six people. Near Jerusalem, Mitzpeh Rachel on Kibbutz Ramat Rachel has a splendid view of Bethlehem and the Judean Desert as well as a swimming pool, tennis courts, and modern convention facilities.

Price includes:
Accommodations, breakfast. You buy lunch and dinner in the kibbutz dining room for $10 to $15. Fly & Drive Hotel vouchers are available for 7 nights at any of the 26 kibbutz hotels.

Sample prices:
$63 single room, one night, regular season, Mitzpeh Rachel
$80 double room, one night, low season, Nof Ginosaur.
$113 double room, on night, high season, Ein Gedi, Dead Sea.

Children:
All ages welcome.

Mobility International
**Box 3551
Eugene OR 97403
Phone: (503)343-1284
Fax: (503)343-6812**

This worldwide organization provides information and encouragement to people with disabilities who want to travel. "Families who are members are welcome to use our information referral service," notes a staff member. "We can tell them where they can find accessible campgrounds or places to stay, and we can answer their questions about traveling with a disabled family member."

The organization has published a book, *World of Options for the 1990s: A Guide to International Exchange, Community Service and Travel for Persons with Disabilities* ($16), a helpful guide for disabled travelers.

Membership:
$20 individuals.
$25 non-profit groups.

"Sure there are obstacles, but it's worth all the trouble."
Quadriplegic exchange student.

Rascals in Paradise
Adventure Express Travel
650 Fifth Street/#505
San Francisco CA 94107
Phone: (415)978-9800/(800)U-RASCAL
Fax:(415)442-0289
Contact: Theresa Detchemendy/Deborah Baratta

Created to specialize in family vacations, this company offers Family Week trips to Mexico, the Caribbean, Jamaica, the Bahamas, Hawaii, and to France, England, Finland, Africa, Papua New Guinea, Galapagos Islands, Fiji, Tahiti, Australia and New Zealand. They also offer ranch vacations in the United States. Their itineraries are designed for three to six families who want to share vacation time with their children.

Their aim is offer vacations that provide "quality, value and fun for each family member." They provide babysitters for families with infants, teacher escorts on small group departures, special sports clinics for parents and teens, and time alone for parents away from the children.

For families who can't join a Family Week schedule, independent itineraries can be arranged.

Price includes:
Accommodations, meals, taxes, babysitting.
Sample trips:
$2,230 per family, hotel room, one week, Akumal, Mexico.
$3,695 2 adults, 2 children 6 to 12, one week, skiing, Telluride.
$3,250 adult, $2,750 children 7 to 18, two weeks, safari, Africa.
Children:
All ages welcome accompanied by parents.

Russian Homestay Program
Home & Host International
2445 Park Avenue
Minneapolis MN 55404
Phone: (612)871-0596/(800)SOVIET U
Fax: (612)871-8853

For 10 days, you live with an English-speaking family in your own private room in Russia. Your host will act as your personal guide to the fascinating sites in the area. You meet your host's family and friends, and gain a personal view of the new Russia of the 1990s.

The Deluxe Homestay is one of the ways you can explore Russia with a Russian family. You can also choose a homestay, or bed and breakfast, a dorm stay, an apartment rental, a special interest pairing with a host, or a homestay with activities such as language study, hiking, sleigh riding in Siberia, or biking in the Baltics. There are also all-inclusive tours of St. Petersburg and Moscow.

The company publishes a newsletter with information and tips from travelers and staff members, and a handbook guide to Russia.

Price includes:
Accommodations, breakfast (depends on place).
Sample prices:
$45 single, $59 double, one night, private bedroom, breakfast, Baltics B&B.

$99 single, $139 double, one night Homestay, host speaks English, one day escorted tour, 3 meals daily, evening activities with host, tickets to one cultural event a week,.

$2,495 adult, 16 days, tour of St. Petersburg and Moscow.
Children:
All ages welcome accompanied by parents.

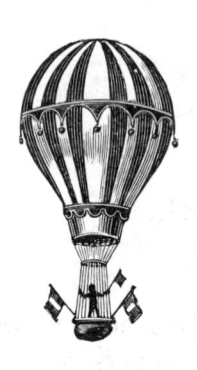

World Learning
Kipling Road
PO Box 676
Brattleboro VT 05302-0676
Phone: (802)257-7751
Fax: (802)258-3248

World Learning is the new name for the US Experiment in International Living, established in 1932, which encouraged learning the language and culture of another country by living as a member of one of its families. World Learning today offers a wide range of travel abroad with a strong educational component.

The Citizen Exchange and Language Programs offer summer vacations abroad, homestay programs, au pairs, Elderhostel, corporate language programs, youth adventure programs, and international high school programs.

Summer Abroad has an extensive list of travel and language programs, ecology adventures, and community service in Africa, Asia, Australia, the Caribbean, Europe and Latin America for students aged 14 to 20, including homestays.

The international high school program sends US students to live in Germany for a year while a student from Germany spends a year.

The Youth Adventure Camp is for 11 to 15-year-olds from around the world. Located in Florida, the summer camp blends language training, recreation and cultural information with time for relaxation on the beach and a visit to Disney World.

Price includes:
Airfare, orientation, accommodations, all meals, transportation, excursions, admission fees, insurance, application fee.
Sample trip:
$2,700 for language study, Mexico.
$3,200 for homestay, France.
$4,800 for ecology adventure, Australia.
Children:
Most programs are designed for over 18.

RANCHES AND COWBOYS

RECIPE FOR COWBOY COFFEE:
1. Take two pounds of grounds
2. Put in enough water to wet it down.
3. Boil for two hours.
4. Throw in a horseshoe.

If the shoe sinks, she ain't ready.

Western dude ranches are working cattle ranches that welcome visitors - called dudes - as guests in the summer. Some ranches have quit the cattle business to concentrate full-time on guests, but at others, you meet real working cowboys while you vacation.

Ranches offer the warmth of genuine hospitality and relaxed friendliness, and the opportunity to explore some of the most beautiful scenery in the country. Most ranches are set on miles of open land with magnificent views of distant mountain peaks and across rolling plains. You can spend a week at ranches in Colorado, Arizona, Utah, Montana, Wyoming, Idaho, Texas, and California as well as in Wisconsin, Pennsylvania, and New York. Some places stay open year-round to offer cross-country skiing, ice-fishing, and snowmobiling in winter.

WHAT'S A RANCH VACATION LIKE?

You'll find that ranches are comfortable, easy-going places, designed to please families of all ages on vacation. While horse-riding is the main focus of activity with guided trail rides every day, you can also fish in the streams, hike in the mountains, swim in the pool, enjoy meals in a comfortable dining room, soak in the hot tub and count the clouds, bask in the sun, and meet other families. Evening activities include square dances, movies, games, rodeos, and barbecues.

For parents, one of the most attractive aspects of a well-run ranch is the child-care program. There's day care for toddlers, group activities for school-age children, and special events for the teenagers, such as water polo games or rodeos.

You won't be roughing it. You'll stay in clean, modern, country-style rooms in the main house or a log cabin with queen-size beds, private bathrooms, and heaters for cool evenings. Most rooms don't have radios, TV, or telephones, so you can get away from it all.

Fresh, home-cooked meals are served in an informal dining room with portions designed to conquer any diet. Most ranches provide a big communal living room with armchairs, sofas, and a huge fireplace for their guests to relax. There's often a library or quiet area for reading, a games room with pool and table tennis, and a social center with music and snacks.

Cattle Round-Ups

Secret cowboys can sign up for a genuine cattle drive. Traditionally, cowboys move cattle down to winter pastures in the fall and take them up to summer pastures in the spring. But there's such a demand for cattle rides after the success of the movie *City Slickers* that some ranchers now move herds of cattle from field to field along a dusty trail every week for the benefit of their visitors who want to share the experience.

On Colorado's western slope, you can join a one-day family cattle ride to move a herd of longhorns about 7 miles along a dusty trail. You start out in the morning with instructions: no

> "It's our annual family get-together. My husband's mother flies in to spend the week with us, and next week my mother arrives from New Jersey. At home, the children are busy with school and we're at work. Here there's time to talk."
>
> *Linda, husband, and two sons from Missouri.*

RANCHES AND COWBOYS

GEAR FOR A CATTLE DRIVE:
1 pair riding boots with heel
1 pair sneakers or hiking shoes
6 pair high cotton socks
5 cotton shirts, long sleeve
2 flannel shirts, long sleeve
2 T-shirts, short sleeve
1 warm lined jacket
1 sweater
3 pair jeans
1 bandana
1 hat with wide brim
1 windbreaker
Sleepwear
Bathing suit
Towels
Toiletries
Work gloves
Long raincoat or rain suit
Flashlight
Canteen
Sunglasses
Sunscreen/lip balm
3-season sleeping bag
Sleeping pad

cantering, and stay either in back of the herd or along the side to discourage the strays. Non-riders can choose to sit in the wagon, and listen to a tape of cowboy and country-western songs to set the ambience. Along the way, you'll stop for a barbecue lunch with steak, chicken, and homemade pie. Then you keep right on riding until you get the cattle to the end of the trail, and come back dusty and exhausted.

In Wyoming, you can join a re-enactment of a weeklong 1800s period cattle drive, camping out along the way with no nylon tents, no pick-ups and no pre-packaged food. You ride with the cowboys on a 35-mile drive to move the cattle to their seasonal grazing grounds. The ranch also invites dudes to join their regular cattle drives during the summer.

GETTING READY

Take time to do a little research before you decide on the ranch to visit. A few questions to ask are:

How many people will be there? Some ranches take 100 people or more. Others can only accommodate about 30 people. You decide if you'd like a place with more people and amenities or a smaller place with a more intimate atmosphere. Both can be fun.

What kind of riding program is there? For beginners, there's usually instruction the first day. Some places assign you a horse for the week, and expect you'll ride every day. At others, you can ride different horses and join a trail ride when you feel like it. Check if the cost of riding is included in the weekly rate or if you pay extra for any riding that you do. You decide which is best: if your family doesn't want to ride every day, it may be less expensive to pay for individual rides.

"People who decide to come for three days always end up wishing they could stay longer."

Ranch Wrangler

What other activities are offered? Is there a swimming pool, guided hikes, rafting trips, cookouts, overnight camping, nature walks? Don't hesitate to ask about your particular interests - ranch owners can direct you to prehistoric Indian cave dwellings or nature preserves.

How long can we stay? Usually ranches expect a minimum stay of one week, but some offer three-day and four-day options, and even weekend stays. Many ranches are often booked up months ahead so don't wait too long to make a reservation.

What kinds of accommodations are available? You'll find a choice of cabins, lodge rooms, and suites available, with twin, double, queen and king-size beds. A family group of three couples and two children can stay in a three-bedroom cabin with two bathrooms, a living room and porch set in the woods a short stroll from the main lodge. A couple with two children may prefer a cabin bedroom suite with living room and bath, or a room in the main lodge close to the dining room and evening activities.

What's the food like? Ranches provide three meals a day, with a full breakfast, often served buffet style, lunch or picnic lunch to take with you, and complete dinner. Menus vary from ranch to ranch. Often, there's a barbecue outdoors and an overnight camping trip. A breakfast ride serves a cookout at the end of the trail. If you need a special diet, discuss it before you arrive.

What's the location? It's a good idea to check the altitude if you're coming from sea level. You may need a day or so to get used to the thinner air at ranches high in the mountains, over 7,000 feet or so. Other ranches may be in exceptionally dry or dusty places, or be near a lake with a bunch of hungry mosquitoes around. Remember that the higher you go, the cooler the temperatures, so don't forget a sweater.

WITH CHILDREN
Babies and Toddlers

Every ranch has facilities for children. Many offer full-time day care, and planned programs of activities for toddlers. Ask if the pool has a shallow end or special children's area for splashing and playing in the water. Check if there are pony rides for toddlers. Some places have separate children's dining rooms so parents can eat on their own.

Youngsters and Teenagers

Once children are old enough to sit on a horse, they will find plenty to do and make friends with other children on trail rides and other activities. Check if there's a recreation room with table tennis or pinball games for teens, and what special evening activities are planned for them.

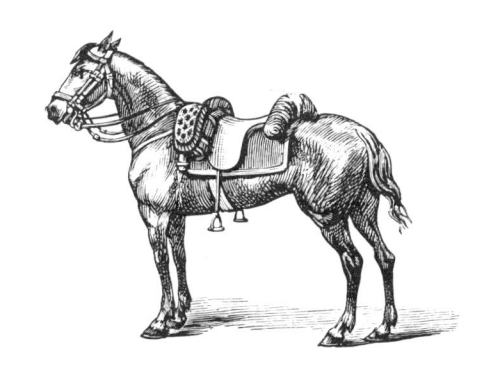

RESOURCE GUIDE TO RANCHES

American Wilderness Experience
PO Box 1486
Boulder CO 80306
Phone: (303)444-2622/(800)444-0099
Fax: (303)444-3999
Contact: Dave Wiggins, President

AWE is a clearinghouse and central reservation office for dozens of ranches in the United States as well as for adventure travel trips including llama treks, snowmobile tours, hiking, river rafting, fishing, canoeing, mountain biking, cross-country skiing, sailing, and kayaking.

AWE publishes an annual guide to Western Dude Ranch Vacations that includes maps, photographs, and complete descriptions of dude ranches in the West with prices, how many guests, facilities, and riding programs.

"We like people to call and tell us what they're looking for and then we can suggest a vacation that's just right for their needs," says Dave Wiggins. "We're here to prescribe the ideal antidote for the stress and craziness of an over-civilized world!"

Price includes:
Accommodations, all meals, equipment, guides, instruction, all activities.

Sample trips:
$630 adult, $285 children 7 to 12, $180 children 2 to 6, one week, ranch in Arizona.
$699 adult, $599 children under 12, one week, ranch in Montana.
$810 adult, $550 children 6 to 9, one week, ranch in Colorado.

Children:
All ages welcome.

FIRST DAY ON A DUDE RANCH

"I'm sitting astride a sturdy brown horse called Brandy, following a line of horses along a tree-shaded trail. We're climbing up and I can see the white peaks of mountains silhouetted against the blue sky ahead. It's the first time I've tried horse riding in my life, and it feels great!"

**Cheyenne River Ranch
1031 Steinle Road
Douglas WY 82633
Phone: (307)358-2380
Fax: (307)358-4454
Contact: Don & Betty Pellatz**

The Pellatz' ranch stands amid Wyoming's Thunder Basin National Grassland north of Douglas, 8,000 acres of rolling hills covered with sagebrush, grass, and cactus. The land stretches for miles under open skies, and at night the stars are spectacular.

This is an authentic working ranch where the family runs both cattle and sheep. Don and Betty Pellatz and their five children take only a few guests. You'll share all aspects of ranch life.

Six times between May and October you can help the family move cattle to different ranges, riding along the dusty trails, through large groves of cottonwoods, across dry cactus-studded flats, and into areas filled with knee-deep golden grass. Overnight, you camp out or go back to the ranch. The next day you trail the herd to their new pastures.

Price includes:
Accommodations, all meals, horse riding.
Sample prices:
$475 adult, $350 children under 12, one week.
$85 adult, $60 children, daily rate.
Children:
All ages welcome.

ROUND-UP

"On Saturday we rounded up the cattle and spent the night at the ranch. On Sunday till Friday we drove the cattle about 60 miles across land and camped out. The scenery is unbelievable. I have seen antelope, deer, rabbits, eagles, and wild turkey. We really have had a truly amazing experience."

Visitors from England.

Colorado Dude & Guest Ranch Association
PO Box 300
Tabernash CO 80478
Phone: (303)724-3653/(303)887-3128
Contact: Wright Catlow, Executive Director

The association publishes an annual free directory with descriptions of CDGRA members' ranches, details of prices, activities, facilities and number of guests. The ranches have been personally visited and inspected by Wright Catlow, Executive Director, CDGRA, and meet the standards of quality and service required by the association.

The directory includes photos, a map to locate ranches and a well-designed grid table for easy comparison so you can decide if you'd like to go to a summer ranch with 24 guests, a pool, tennis, and hunting, or a year-round ranch with room for 110 with babysitting, guided hikes, pack trips, and river rafting. Call for your free copy.

Member ranches of CDRGA are listed at the end of this chapter, and you can contact them directly for free information.

Dude Ranchers Association
PO Box 471
LaPorte CO 80535
Phone: (303)223-8440

This association, founded in 1926, publishes an annual magazine and directory ($3) describing dude ranch vacations at members' ranches in Wyoming, Montana, Colorado, and other Western states including Texas and South Dakota. The 100 entries have descriptions of the ranches, and a map to show where they are located. The publication includes articles, letters, and photographs about ranching vacations.

You can call the Association at 1-900-535-9700, Ext. 634 for a two-minute message of general information about dude ranch vacations.

High Island Guest Ranch
PO Box 71-1
Hamilton Dome WY 82427
Winter: Box 7, Fryeburg ME 04031
Phone: (307)867-2374/Winter(207)925-3285
Fax: (207)925-3096
Contact: Susan Eastman

This working cattle ranch invites families to spend a week riding to their hearts' content in the 41,000 acres of prairies and mountains. Trails take you to discover ancient petroglyphs chipped into rock cliffs, remnants of an ancient tepee ring site of the Great Plains Indians, a ride overlooking the 12,800-foot Washakie Needles, and an overnight trail ride to the mountains and the Upper Lodge.

You can work with the cowboys on weeklong cattle drives in the 1800s period style, or one of the authentic cattle drives still common today. The drives are in July, August and September. There are also branding weeks, round-ups, and photo safaris and you can help with daily cowboy chores. Every week ends with a celebration barbecue and entertainment.

Price includes:
Accommodations, all meals, instruction, horses, tack, saddlebags, canvas trail bag.

Sample trips:
$995 adult, $695 children 12 to 15, one week, round-up weeks.
$1,095 adult, $795 children 12 to 15, one week, Authentic Drive.
$1,495 anyone 16 or older, one week, 1800s Cattle Drive.

Children:
12 and over welcome. 16 and over, Cattle Drive.

PROMISE
"You may arrive as a city slicker but you will leave as a cowboy after a week riding the range."

Susan Eastman.

Rocky Mountain Cattle Moovers
PO Box 457
Carbondale CO 81623
Phone: (303)963-9666

If you'd like a short cattle drive experience, this is the trip to take. No horse riding experience necessary - the horses are only allowed to walk. Wear comfortable clothes. You don't need cowboy boots - sneakers are fine. You can also choose to ride in the wagon.

Daylong cattle drives are offered throughout the summer. The Big 4 Ranch is near Carbondale on Colorado's western slope, but vans pick up participants in Glenwood Springs and Carbondale. The ride starts about 9 a.m. and returns about 4 p.m. Monday through Saturday.

Price includes:
Transportation, steak lunch, raingear, hats, bandanas, soft drinks, breakfast, snack, water, instruction.

Sample trip:
$160 adult, children 14 and older, horse ride.
$120 children 7 to 13, horse ride.
$65, adult, children 7 and older, wagon ride.

Children:
Accepted at 7 and older.

"We had the best family vacation we've ever experienced. Our three boys said it was better than Disney World, and that's the best kind of accolade coming from them."

Family from Alabama.

Wilderness Trails Ranch
776 County Road 300
Durango CO 81301
Phone: (303)247-0722/(800)527-2624
Fax: (303)247-1006
Contact: Gene or Jan Roberts

Cattle Round-ups have been part of the action here for several years. Every September, 16 visitors or Herdbusters join the ranchers in bringing 220 cattle - mother cows, calves and bulls - out of the high country surrounding Wilderness Trail. The ranch also offers an annual Wilderness Caballeros Week with 16 riders who take day rides and move a few cattle along the way. Book early! There's a waiting list for these programs.

Owners Gene and Jan Roberts have been at the ranch in southwestern Colorado for 23 years. You'll find plenty of horses to ride, and instruction for those who need it. Join daily rides for different levels in small groups, and a weekly Family Ride to a scenic spot. Trails lead across sunlit meadows with blue spruce and aspen trees, up to the cliffs at Vista Grande, and through shady woods. Nearby, Vallecito Lake offers waterskiing, and there's great fishing in the creeks near the lodge. In the evenings, you can try western swing dancing, be entertained by the weekly staff show, or enjoy the campfire sing-a-longs or an overnight campout.

Price includes:
Accommodations, all meals, horse riding, activities, excursions, guides, instruction.

Sample prices:
$950 adult, Sunday to Sunday, Cattle Round-up and Caballeros Week.
$975 adult, Sunday to Sunday, on ranch.
Children: 12 to 17, $795. 6 to 11, $725. 4 to 5, $625. 2 to 3, $520. Under 2, free.

Children:
All ages welcome. No child care for under 2.

COLORADO DUDE AND GUEST RANCH ASSOCIATION MEMBERS

Contact the ranches directly for free information.

ASPEN CANYON RANCH
13206 County Road #3,
Star Route
Parshall CO 80468.
Phone: (800)321-1357
Contact: The Mitchells

ASPEN LODGE RANCH RESORT
6120 Highway 7
Longs Peak Route
Estes Park CO 80517
Phone: (800)332-MTNS
Contact: Tom & Jill Hall

BAR LAZY J GUEST RANCH
Box ND
Parshall CO 80468
Phone: (303)725-3437
Contact: Larry & Barbara Harmon

CHEROKEE PARK RANCH
Box 97
Livermore CO 80536
Phone: (800)628-0949
Contact: B. & Eli Elfland

C LAZY U RANCH
Box 379-D
Granby CO 80446
Phone: (303)887-3344
Contact: The Clark Murray Family

COLORADO TRAILS RANCH
26 County Road 240-W
Durango CO 81301
Phone: (800)323-DUDE
Contact: Dick & Ginny Elder

COULTER LAKE GUEST RANCH
Box 906
Rifle CO 81650
Phone: (800)858-3046
Contact: Norm & Sue Benzinger

DEER VALLEY RANCH
Box E
Nathrop CO 81236
Phone: (719)395-2353
Contact: John Woolmington/ Harold DeWalt

DIAMOND J GUEST RANCH
26604 Frying Pan Road
Meredith CO 81642
Phone: (303)927-3222
Contact: Martha & Bill Sims

DON K. RANCH
2677 S. Siloam Road
Pueblo CO 81005
Phone: (800)874-0307
Contact: Smith Family

RANCHES AND COWBOYS 135

FRIENDSHIP

"The one underlying principle that sets us apart from other types of vacations is that you are a guest in the owner ranchers' home. This makes our type of vacation something that really can't be duplicated by the many resorts out there. The one most enduring reward of our Dude Ranch vacation experience, and the one that sets us apart, are the people we serve and the friendships that just seem to happen here at the ranch."

*Ken and Randy Sue Fosha,
Drowsy Water Ranch, Colorado.*

DROWSY WATER RANCH
Box 147A
Granby CO 80446
Phone: (800)845-2292
Contact: Ken & Randy Sue Fosha

ELK MOUNTAIN RANCH
Box 910
Buena Vista CO 81211
Phone: (719)395-6313
Contact: Tom & Sue Murphy

FOCUS RANCH
Slater CO 81653
Phone: (303)583-2410
Contact: Terry Reidy

4UR RANCH
Box 340 D
Creede CO 81130
Phone: (719)658-2202
Contact: Rock & Kristen Swanson

THE FRYINGPAN RIVER RANCH
32042 Fryingpan Road
Meredith CO 81642
Phone: (303)927-3570
Contact: Jim Rea

HARMEL'S RANCH RESORT
Box 944
Gunnison CO 81230
Phone: (800)235-3402
Contact: Brad Milner

THE HOME RANCH
Box 8221
Clark CO 80248
Phone: (303)879-9044
Contact: Ken Jones

LAKE MANCOS RANCH
Box 2061A
Durango CO 81302
Phone: (800)325-WHOA
Contact: The Sehnert Family

LATIGO RANCH
Box 237
Kremmling CO 80459
Phone: (800)227-9655
Contact: Yost & George Families

LAZY H GUEST RANCH
Box 248
Allenspark CO 80510
Phone: (800)578-3598
Contact: Phil & Karen Olbert

LOST VALLEY RANCH
Route 2, Box 70
Sedalia CO 80135
Phone: (303)647-2311/2495
Contact: The Bob Foster Famliies

NORTH FORK RANCH
Box B
Shawnee CO 80475
Phone:(800)843-7895
Contact: Dean & Karen May

OLD GLENDEVY RANCH
Glendevey,
Colorado Route,
Jelm WY 82063
Phone: (303)435-5701
Contact: Garth & Olivia Peterson

PEACEFUL VALLEY LODGE &
RANCH RESORT
Box 2811 Star Route
Lyons CO 80540
Phone: (303)747-2881
Contact: Mabel Boehm

THE PINES RANCH
Box 311
Westcliffe CO 81252
Phone: (800)446-WHOA
Contact: Dean & Casey Rusk

POWDERHORN GUEST RANCH
Powderhorn CO 81243
Phone: (800)786-1220
Contact: Jim & Bonnie Cook

RAINBOW TROUT RANCH
Box 249
Winter Park CO 80482
Phone: (800)633-3397
Contact: Director

RANCH ON SWEETWATER
2650 Sweetwater Road
Gypsum CO 81637
Phone: (800)321-7639
Contact: Wing/Gates Famlies

RAWAH RANCH
Glendevey Colorado Route C
Jelm WY 82063
Phone: (303)435-5715
Contact: Pete & Ardy Kunz

SAN JUAN GUEST RANCH
2882 Highway 23
Ridgway CO 81432
Phone: (800)331-3015
Contact: Pat, Scott & Cristy MacTiernan

7W GUEST RANCH
3412 County Road 151
Gypsum CO 81637
Phone: (800)524-1286
Contact: Missy Taylor

SKY CORRAL RANCH
8233 Old Flowers Road
Bellvue CO 80512
Phone: (303)484-1362
Contact: Vannices/Anderson Familiies

SKYLINE GUEST RANCH
Box 67
Telluride CO 81435
Phone: (303)728-3757
Contact: The Farny Family

SYLVAN DALE GUEST RANCH
2939 N. County Road 31D
Loveland CO 80538
Phone: (303)667-3915
Contact: The Jessup Family

TUMBLING RIVER RANCH
Box 30
Grant CO 80448
Phone: (800)654-8770
Contact: Jim & Mary Dale Gordon

VISTA VERDE GUEST & SKI
TOURING RANCH
Box 465
Steamboat Springs CO 80477
Phone: (800)526-RIDE
Contact: John & Suzanne Munn

WAUNITA HOT SPRINGS
RANCH
8007 County Road 887
Box 3
Gunnison CO 81230
Phone: (303)641-1266
Contact: The Pringle Family

WHISTLING ACRES GUEST
RANCH
Box 88CD
Paonia CO 81428
Phone: (800)346-1420
Contact: Jerry & Roberta Bradley

WILDERNESS TRAILS RANCH
776 County Road 300
Box A
Durango CO 81301
Phone: (303)247-0722
Contact: Gene & Jan Roberts

WIND RIVER RANCH
Box 3410 D
Estes Park CO 80517
Phone: (800)523-4212
Contact: Rob & Jere Irvin

FAVORITE TIME

"One of my favorite times is dinner. We had our table by the window, and we could look out at the sun setting behind the mountains. There'd be a buffet with salad or a choice of fish, chicken or meat, with soup, rolls, and dessert. We'd all talk about what we'd done that day, and even our 3-year-old had a story of riding on a pony in the corral, led by her sister. I've never square danced in my life but we ended up doing the do-si-dos."

*Susan from Boston
at ranch with her three daughters.*

138 *FAMILY TRAVEL*

SKI AND SNOW
BY CLAIRE WALTER

A family ski vacation, like parenthood itself, can be one of life's most memorable and satisfying adventures or a potent argument for celibacy. The right place at the right time will offer the experience that makes a lifetime of wonderful memories.

Skiing is the ideal family sport, and ski resorts—more than any other category of travel provider—go the extra mile to make families welcome with kids ski and/or stay free offers and facilities and programs to provide an enjoyable experience for all. It's an activity people of all ages and various ability levels can share. Little ones as young as three can slide down a gentle slope, ride a lift and feel part of the world of big people. School-age youngsters with just a little mileage under their ski bottoms can cruise all over the mountain, being out in the crisp fresh air and participating in a sport that is individual, social, and just plain fun.

Teens on skis or snowboards have developed a healthy on-slope culture that chases the winter blues. Some become ardent "shredders"—riders of snowboards are related more to surfboards than to skis—while others take up racing or freestyle skiing with the passion of youth. For adults, skiing's lures are potent—adventure, scenery, physical activity, good companionship. And grandparents can join in the fun for a pittance, because most ski areas offer sharply reduced or even free lift tickets to seniors over 60, 65, or 70.

WHAT'S A SKI VACATION LIKE?

Families can ski together as long as the faster members are willing to wait for the slower ones. People of different ability levels can ski different runs off the same lift and meet at the bottom for the ride up. In short, it's an individual sport that everyone can share, depending on each other for companionship but not for the success of a particular turn or the joy of a particular run.

Ski Schools

Good ski schools have especially endearing children's ski facilities. Instructors are those who love children and relate best to them. The combination of ski time, indoor play time, and snack and meal breaks depend on the groups' age, stamina, and ability level, as well as the weather, and experienced instructors know just how to balance the day so that their charges get the most from the experience.

Beginners: The smallest beginners are normally taught on a small, gentle hill—often fenced off. A little skier (say, ages 3 or 4 to 6) needs a ski school that combines on-snow and indoor play and rest time that makes the day satisfying and fun. Sometimes there's a little lift or tow; other times children sidestep up a carpet.

Children quickly progress to a "terrain garden." These can be as simple as a few cartoon cut-outs stuck in the snow and perhaps the snow itself sculpted into bumps, troughs and mini-moguls to give youngsters the feeling of weight control, edging and other skiing skills. At bigger resorts, they can be complex ski-through theme parks, with elaborate structures on mining,

---

CHILDREN'S NEEDS

"Instructors today not only need to teach skiing, they also need to know where a child is in terms of physical, mental and social abilities. They need to understand a child's limitations."

*Paul Mundy, director
Professional Ski Instructors Assn.*

Indian, Western, or other popular motifs. Even older children, who don't need such facilities, adore skiing through them whenever they have the chance.

Older children: Because it is a sport that lasts a lifetime, an introduction to the skiing world is one of the best gifts parents can bestow on their children. And for parents themselves, the memories of skiing and ski vacationing together last forever.

Some people like to ski with their older children, while others prefer to put them into ski school. Since teaching one's own child a sport is probably the world's second-worst idea, right after teaching a spouse how to drive, this is a good tactic for beginners. A youngster of about 7 to 12 needs classes geared to his or her ability to learn fast and keep going.

Teens: Even teens who have been skiing since they were tykes (and may outrun their parents) often benefit immeasurably from fast-moving classes, usually taught by hot young instructors who aren't too far out of their teens themselves and won't spend a lot of time talking or drawing pictures in the snow with a pole tip.

How to Choose Where to Go and Where to Stay

Ski vacations have two parameters—the "ski" part (lifts, ski slopes and ski schools) and the "vacation" part (lodging, dining and entertainment). The place a family chooses must suit the needs of everyone involved. In this age of his/hers/theirs families, two-career couples with awesome schedules to juggle, and astonishingly sophisticated children who are equally at home in the air, on the slopes, and under a palm tree, the decision on where to go can be tough.

In reality, there's no single "best" family ski resort, but ski country is full of alternatives that are right for different needs. A

NEW PARENTS

"We carefree singles of twenty years ago have become 'family units,' eagerly pursueing careers, home life and parenthood. And, of course, we're taking our kids with us when we go to the mountains."

Ski parent from California.

place suitable for a couple toting an infant may not be right for a family with lively school-age children or with hard-skiing, vaguely anti-social teenagers. Still, there are some general parameters.

Adults, who after all are paying the freight, really are entitled to have the kind of skiing experience that they would select if they were skiing solo, still keeping in mind that the success or failure of a ski vacation can ultimately hinge on how suitable a place is for the children. If there's an infant or pre-skier, there must be a convenient, congenial nursery for both the child and the parents to be happy.

Skiing is the force that drives the vacation—and the terrain truly ought to be right for everyone. But beyond this, the choice of vacation spots also depends on many other factors.

Picking The Right Place

The ideal resort will have three key advantages:

1. It will be within driving distance of home or reasonably close to an airport.

2. It will have commodious lodging. Condos are usually preferred by skiing families for their spaciousness, ability to offer privacy, and availability of kitchen and laundry facilities.

3. The daily commute between the lodging and the slopes will be easy (i.e., very short walk or frequent, free shuttle bus). If there's a bus stop close to both your lodging and the door to nursery and children's ski school, so much the better. Even a family that drives to the resort in its own car or a rental vehicle is wise to take the shuttle to the lifts rather than hassling with looking for a place to park every morning.

Finding a good place to stay means asking the right questions.

Is the lodge slopeside, within walking distance of the lifts, or accessible by shuttle bus? Slopeside implies ski-in, ski-out convenience, but what is within walking distance for an older child or adult might not be for a little one, especially after a busy day of skiing and playing. Most Western destination resorts run shuttle buses on a regular, frequent and equitable schedule.

Are there things to do besides skiing? Whether you prefer a condo, a hotel or a casual lodge, you'll want to make sure there are ample opportunities for children to amuse themselves after the lifts shut down. The availability of a swimming pool or game room is a real plus for school-age children, and a compact, car-free resort where they can roam with their buddies is desirable. Larger ski resorts are trickier, but when there's an organized children's evening, enabling adults to slip away for a child-free dinner, even the most sophisticated ski town can become a family-pleaser.

Is there a central reservations service? You'll find a list of toll-free 800 numbers at the end of the chapter. Make sure to ask about anything you need to know. They are a goldmine of specific information about nurseries, children's ski schools, accommodations, and the general resort layout.

If you're seeking the perfect ski resort, here are some questions to ask.

Can I bring my 6-months-old baby? It depends on how young a baby the nursery will accept. At Sugarloaf, Maine, it's 6 weeks; at Crested Butte, CO, it's 6 months. At Crystal Mountain, WA, infants are accepted midweek but not weekends. Ask about provision for nursing mothers. Steamboat, CO, has a ski-in doorway directly from the slopes.

Is there a nursery for my 2-year-old? Find out what is the ratio of care-givers to charges (1 adult to 3 to 5 infants and 1 adult to 6 to 10 toddlers are the usual ranges). Are reservations required, requested, or recommended? Is a deposit necessary? Is it refundable if someone comes down with the chicken pox and you have to cancel? Is lunch included in the nursery cost or available at additional cost? Parents are usually asked to bring baby food and formula, but most nurseries serve such kid classics as PB&J, hot dogs, grilled cheese, and burgers for nursery and ski school attendees—unless you make other arrangements.

Where is the nursery located? Since provisioning a baby for a day approximates outfitting an expedition across Antarctica, parents who must tote bundled baby plus a supply of diapers, bottles, baby food, and a couple of changes of clothing—PLUS their own gear—appreciate convenience. This is all the more true for those who live at sea level and are doing all that lugging at 7,000 feet or higher. In Colorado, Keystone's nursery is just steps along flat pavement from the shuttle-bus stop; at Steamboat and Vail's Lionshead, it's necessary to navigate stairs and busy pedestrian plazas.

What facilities are there for my child who's starting skiing? Ask if ski equipment and lift tickets are included in the cost of children's lessons, as they often are for children under 6. Ask if you can store rental equipment in the children's center. When my son, then 5, attended Steamboat's children's ski school, we had the choice of carting his equipment to the ski check in one direction or our condo in the other each afternoon; the facility has since been expanded.

Where is the rental shop? In Winter Park, CO, there's an outstanding children's facility that wisely features the kids' rental shop right on premises. So does Smugglers' Notch, VT. At Mt. Snow, VT, the children's ski school and rental shop are on two floors of the same building.

PARENT PRESSURE
"An anxious mother repeatedly came to check on the progress of her 4-year-old daughter during her first day's lessons in ski school. Finally her daughter looked up and asked impatiently, "Don't you have your own school to go to?""

My child knows how to ski so can he go off with his friends? You want to know if the ski terrain is easy to figure out. It's a lot less problematic for a family to rendezvous at Grand Targhee, WY, Purgatory, CO, or Taos, NM, where everything funnels back to one base than at Vail with three major egresses from the slopes or Heavenly Valley, CA; Park City, UT; Sun Valley, ID; or Telluride, CO, with two.

Are there things for 12-year-olds to do with their friends? Ask if the resort is self-contained, if the health club and/or swimming pool admits unsupervised youngsters, if there's a good bus system that runs into the evening for children ready to use it by themselves. See if there's a supervised facility with non-alcoholic beverages, games, and other youngsters. Steamboat, Vail, and Winter Park are Colorado resorts that provide these facilities, as does Vermont's Bolton Valley and Stowe.

What about teenagers who don't want to ski with the family? Several places provide ski classes for teens. They are offered at least during holidays at such resorts as Killington, VT; Snowmass, CO; Mammoth, CA; Sugarbush, VT; Taos, NM; Telluride, CO, and Waterville Valley, NH. They're not cheap, but it may be worth gold to know what active youngsters are up to.

What can teenagers do in the evening? You need to know if there's a good health spa, swimming pool, or tennis center that teens can use. What about a movie theater? A skating rink? A couple of alcohol-free burger or pizza joints where teens hang out? Maybe there's some sort of organized, age-appropriate evening program, or at least a discreetly supervised teen center? Is it one your child will be willing to go to? If your answer to either of these questions is no, then you might prefer to let youngsters loose in a compact resort where they can't get into too much trouble.

Finding Family Ski Deals

Despite skiing's image as an expensive sport, freebies for families abound. Steamboat, CO, pioneered Kids Ski Free in 1982, and in the following decade, about 100,000 children 12 and under have enjoyed free skiing, lodging, and even rental equipment on a one-on-one basis with their parents.

Similar programs now blanket the country like snowflakes. Most ski areas offer free skiing to children to age 5 or 6 (Michigan's Boyne Mountain and Boyne Highlands extend it through age 9), and free skiing and/or lodging for youngsters has spread to resorts across the land as well, normally except during Christmas/New Year and President's Week vacation periods.

While most ski areas sell children's lift tickets to age 12, charging adult rates thereafter, some stretch what they consider a child: Welch Mountain and Wild Mountain, MN, and Big Tupper, NY, to 17; Spirit Mountain, MN, and Black Mountain, NH, to 15; Cranmore, NH, Bromley and Pico, VT, and Jackson Hole, WY, to 14, and Winter Park, CO, Cannon Mountain, NH, Butternut Basin, MA, and Sugarbush, VT, to 13.

Others offering "student," "youth," or "junior" tickets between adult and child prices include such larger areas as Bear Mountain and Snow Summit, CA; The Big Mountain, MT; Mission Ridge, WA; Sandia Peak, NM; Big Powderhorn, Blackjack, and Indianhead on Michigan's Upper Peninsula, and Highmount, NY. It's usually designed for the junior high and high school years, but Waterville Valley, NH's student ticket is good for ages 13 to 20 with a valid school or college ID.

Other innovative ticket pricing helps families too. Rope tows are free at Bogus Basin, ID, while Okemo, VT, has two free beginner lifts. Cascade Mountain's Schoolmarm section is free. Winter Park, CO, charges just $3 a day for any skier to use the

Galloping Goose beginner lift and $15 for adults and $10 for children for a Mini-Mountain ticket, good on five lifts and 200 acres of mostly novice and intermediate terrain.

Nursery Care: While nursery care is usually costly, some resorts even have good deals in that department too. Jay Peak, VT, offers free child care for 2-year-olds and up anytime between 9 a.m. to 9 p.m. to families staying at the Hotel Jay or in a resort condominium. Okemo, VT, provides free midweek child care before Christmas and from late March to the end of the ski season. They used to offer it most of the winter, but demand was so great that the nursery was "free but full," according to Okemo's Scott Van Pelt. Waterville Valley offers the option of skiing or nursery care for children on three- to five-day non-holiday midweek packages.

Claire Walter is Western editor of *Skiing* magazine, editor of the *Berlitz Handbook to Skiing the Alps*, and author of the award-winning *The Best Ski Resorts in America*, and *Rocky Mountain Skiing*. She skis with her son, Andrew.

RESOURCE GUIDE TO SKIING VACATIONS

When planning a ski vacation, pay careful attention to resorts providing free lift tickets and/or accommodations for youngsters. Lodging is often restricted to a resort's own properties or at least participating properties in a nearby town. Children usually must share their parents' room or condo. Rates are based on double occupancy for any size unit. Lifts, lodging, and/or other services are usually free on the basis of one child per paying adult. Unless noted otherwise, the offer is valid for youngsters to age 12.

Copper Mountain
PO Box 3001
Copper Mountain CO 80443
Phone: 800-458-8386
Children:
Can ski and stay free. Free breakfast and dinner, O'Shea's Restaurant.

Crested Butte
PO Box A,
Mt. Crested Butte CO 81225
Phone: (800)544-8448
Children:
Can ski free. Call for details.

Diamond Peak
1210 Ski Way
Incline Village NV 89451
Phone: (800)TAHOE-4-U
Children:
18 and under, ski and stay free. 3-day, 3-night minumum.

Grand Targhee
PO Box SKI,
Alta WY 83422
Phone: (800)TARGHEE
Children:
Can ski and stay free with 3-day, 3-night minimum. Also free airport transfers.

Purgatory/Durango
PO Box 666,
Durango, CO 81301
Phone: (800)525-9892
Children;
Can ski and stay free every day, including holiday weeks.

Schweitzer
PO Box 815,
Sandpoint, ID 83864
Phone: (800)831-8810
Canada: (800)544-4933
Children:
Can ski and stay free with 4-day, 4-night minumum stay.

Snowbird
Snowbird UT 84902
Phone: (800)453-3000
Children:
　Can ski and stay free all season long. No minimum stay. At least one adult skier in lodging.

Steamboat
2305 Mt. Werner Circle
Steamboat Springs CO 80487
Phone: (800)922-2722
Children:
　Can ski and stay free. Also free rental equipment; 5-day minimum.

Stowe Mountain Resort
Mt. Mansfield Road
Stowe VT 05672
Phone: (800)253-4SKI/ (800)24-STOWE
Children:
　Free skiing on 5-day and 7-day packages; half of adult ticket on 3-day packages. Free lesson for each participant.

Sun Valley
Sun Valley ID 83353
Phone: (800)SUN-VALY
Children:
　17 and under ski and stay free. Children 11 and under free at all times.

Waterville Valley
Waterville Valley NH 03223
Phone: (800)468-2553
Children:
　Option of free nursery instead of free skiing. 3-day to 5-day midweek packages.

White Mountains
PO Box 10
North Woodstock NH 03262
Phone: (800)367-3364
Lodgings: (800)WE-SKI-93
White Mts. Info: (800)FIND-MTS
Children:
　5-day midweek Family Pass except Christmas/New Year. Good at Attitash, Balsams/Wilderness, Black, Bretton Woods, Cannon, Cranmore, Loon, Waterville, Wildcat. Some lodgings match free offer.

Ski Resorts in Europe

The ski resorts in the European Alps are best for an independent child who knows how to ski and ride lifts. Particularly in peak season, classes are huge. Surface lifts, often loosely attended, abound, and children aren't given much help getting on and off. Also, infant nurseries are rare, and lessons are normally not available for children under four.

American ski schools group children by age and ability; Europeans by language and ability. The likelihood of instructors fluent in English is greater in Austria and Switzerland, less in France and Italy.

SKIING ABROAD

"In Mayrhofen, Austria, my kindergartner was by far the youngest in a class whose oldest member was 12. He kept up well, because his all-British classmates skied once a year, while he went almost every weekend. On balance, a ski vacation in the Alps is wonderful for an American child."
Parent from Colorado.

Les Arcs, France:
There are 3 car-free villages, an infant nursery, and a hotel with infant nursery and evening supervision. Ski school programs for all from pre-schoolers to teens. Mecca for snowboarders and other new-wave types.

Avoriaz, France:
Compact and car-free. Children's Village with ski lessons from age 3. Club Med Mini-Club, ages 4 to 8.

Courchevel, France:
2 pre-school nurseries, one with outdoor snowplay. Ski lessons for early ages if child is "ready." Under 5, ski free.

Crans-Montana, Switzerland:
Sunny, car-free villages with good access from Geneva. Ski school from 3 up. Many family-oriented hotels and non-ski activities.

Flaine, France:
Car-free village. Family-style hotels, one with free nursery. Lessons from age 3 up.

Innsbruck, Austria:
Best bargain in the Alps. In-town child care for non-skiers. Cultural enrichment for older children.

Kitzbühel, Austria:
Separate children's ski school, run by triple Olympic gold medalist Toni Sailer, gives lessons from age 3 up. Easy access from Munich. Children under 3'6" ski free.

Mayrhofen, Austria:
Top children's ski school. Isolated, gentle A-Horn teaching terrain. Tourist offices organizes daily apres-ski fun for children.

La Plagne, France:
Abundance of nursery programs, including one for infants. Lessons from age 3 up.

TRAVEL AND LEARN

"Travel in the younger sort is a part of education, in the elder a part of experience. He that travels into a country before he hath some entrance into the language goes to school, and not to travel."

Francis Bacon.

A learning vacation? If that sounds like going back to school, think again. Today, education stretches far beyond a classroom. How about taking a course in tracking dinosaurs, music, politics, folk dancing, or archaeology digs? Now is the time to think about what you've always wanted to do and try it.

WHAT ARE LEARNING VACATIONS LIKE?

There are so many choices that it's impossible to give a general description. You can find places for arts and crafts, languages and literature, politics and performances. Try folk-dancing in the Appalachians, or take a crafts workshops in woodworking, blacksmithing or dulcimer playing, quilting and spinning. There are even special trips for grandparents and grandchildren to visit New York, Washington DC, New England, Alaska and Hawaii. Here are some parent-tested ideas.

Meeting Today's Indians

Spend a week living with American Indians in Oklahoma to understand their unique history. Oklahoma Indians represent 67 tribes, 35 of which maintain tribal councils. The trip shows you firsthand the real lives and past traditions of today's American Indians. You sleep in tipis, sample native food, meet with elders, chiefs, artists, musicians, and watch ceremonies and celebrations. A woman participant noted:

"Our journey through western and central Oklahoma began on the shores of Canton Lake, two hours northwest of Oklahoma City on the North Canadian River, an area associated with the Cheyenne and Arapaho tribes. We moved our camp to Seminole, headquarters of the Oklahoma Seminole national, to attend a stomp dance held in honor of Seminole veterans. A stomp dance is akin to a square dance but accompanied by chanted prayers instead of music. Friends and family members stomp rhythmically in a circle, counterclockwise, to chants led by a caller. Then we moved to Anadarko where we camped on grounds sometimes used by the Black Leggings Society, a select group of Kiowa warriors. From Anadarko we could explore Comanche, Kiowa, Apache, Wichita, and Caddo cultures."

Unique Community

In the southwest corner of New York state, you can attend courses, plays, concerts, and lectures at a resort that also offers time for swimming, hiking and relaxing. Toni and her husband found The Chatauqua Institution some years ago, and the family has been enjoying vacations there every summer.

"This is one of the most special places on earth!" enthused Toni. "It's like going back 50 years or so and rediscovering a quieter, gentler world. This is a Victorian community with close-together houses, most of which have broad porches where people sit, eat their meals, relax, and socialize. The schedule is structured so that there are separate activities for children and adults, as well as the opportunity to do things together. You'll find classes, seminars and activities literally every hour of the day. Even pre-schoolers ride their bikes along the streets to the camp area."

Art by the Lake

If you love the arts but don't have time to paint, there's an award-winning family summer resort in Wisconsin offering creative workshops on a beautiful lakefront. You'll find dozens of classes in watercolor, oil painting, quilting, carving, and foreign languages, as well as sports classes in sailing, fishing, tennis, and golf. The resort has a lodge and cabins by White Sand Lake, and you can enjoy swimming, boating and hiking as well as brushing up your painting.

Digging into the Past

For dinosaur buffs, there's a summer program where you can look for dinosaur tracks. In Colorado, where some of these huge prehistoric animals once roamed, you work with experts in the field looking for signs of these giant creatures.

Also in Colorado is Crow Canyon Archaeological Center where researchers are trying to discover the remnants of a fascinating Anasazi civilization that disappeared from the Four Corners region of America hundreds of years ago. You work with experts at actual on-site digs.

PREPARATIONS

Decide the kind of educational experience you'd like to share with your family. Here are some questions you may want to ask.

What kind of accommodations are available?
How many people will be there?

Is this program for adults only or are children welcome?
What facilities are there for children?
How long has this program been in operation?
Is there pre-trip orientation?
Do you provide a reading list or preparation materials?
Are academic credits available?
What can other members of my family do here?
How much free time is available?
What outdoor facilities are there?
What kind of entertainment is available?
Are meals included in the price?
Are there any trips or excursions?
Are the instructors qualified?

WITH CHILDREN

Babies and Toddlers: On some educational trips, there's full-time child care available so parents can concentrate on the programs. If that service is not available, the program may not accept very young children.

Youngsters: Many programs welcome school-age children accompanied by parents, and include them in the learning experience. Some programs offer special children's programs.

Teenagers: Can be accepted on most educational programs if they are interested in participating.

RESOURCE GUIDE TO LEARNING VACATIONS

Campbell Folk School
Route 1, Box 14A
Brasstown NC 28902
Phone: (704)837-2775/(800)FOLK-SCH
Fax: (704)837-8637
Contact: Donna

Founded in 1925, this is a unique collaboration between progressive educators inspired by the Folk Schools of rural Denmark and the people of the Appalachian community of Brasstown in North Carolina.

Open year-round, there are classes in Appalachian lap dulcimer, hammered dulcimer, recorder, banjo, guitar and fiddle. Other programs focus on nature and garden instruction, photography, embroidery, woodworking, making corn husk dolls, book binding, quilting, knitting, and more.

Classes run for a full week, a short week, or a weekend. Busy weeks have up to 100 students but typically there are about 60 students. There are free concerts every Friday, community folk dances every other Saturday, and many informal performances by folk musicians and storytellers.

The dining room serves three meals a day, including its famous fresh-baked bread. The school is set in 300 acres of rolling farmland, with no TV or telephones in the rooms.

Price includes:
Tuition. Class materials extra.
Sample prices:
$110, weekend, woodworking Shaker boxes.
$185, 7 days, papermaking.
$205, 8 days, blacksmithing.
Accommodations and meals available.
Children:
Welcome but parents must look after them. Minimum age for classes: 18. Little/Middle Folk School for youngsters in June.

MEET THE ARTS

"For kids who have even the tiniest interest in music, art, dance, theater, or other high-brow stuff, this is the place to get easy exposure."

Parent at Chatauqua.

Chatauqua Institution
Chatauqua NY 14722
Phone:(716)357-6200/(800)836-ARTS
Accommodations: (716)357-6204

This lakeside community, a 750-acre National Historic Landmark, offers a nine-week summer schedule of continuing education, lectures, and religious programming, as well as recreation programs, concerts of all styles of music, opera, and a range of outdoor activities.

Chatauqua began as a summer retreat for Protestant ministers and is now a popular summer community for families of all ages. Children can sign up for different activities each week, and adults choose from an array of classes in the arts, politics, music, and computers to attend. Outdoors, there's swimming, boating and fishing on lake beaches, and tennis, shuffleboard, and golf.

More than 3,000 visitors come every year to choose from over 170 courses on topics ranging from calligraphy to contemporary issues. The faculty of scholars and educators from around the country present seminars on topics such as *Raciscm and Ethnicity, Facts about the Environment* and *Toward a Global Bill of Rights.*

In the evenings, the main amphitheater, which seats 6,000, presents classical music concerts and special events such as jazz and rock, comedy, and musicals.

Weekend and one-week packages that include accommodations, Chatauqua gate tickets, parking, and options for opera and theater tickets are available.

Prices:
Gate Tickets for admission to the grounds and all Amphitheater events. Free on Sunday.

$8.50 Daytime: $17.50 Evening: $38. Weekend: $145. One week. Discounts available for groups of 20 or more.

Theater tickets: $8. Opera tickets $12.50 to $28.00

Children:
Under 12, free general admission.

TRAVEL AND LEARN

Cornell's Adult University
626 Thurston Avenue
Ithaca NY 14850-2490
Phone: (607)255-6260
Fax: (607)255-7533
Contact: Ralph Janis/Director

The summer family program at Cornell is one of the largest and oldest in the country. Started in 1968, it now attracts hundreds of people, about half of whom bring youngsters. Participants come from the United States as well as France, Japan, and Argentina.

Adults attend courses taught by Cornell faculty on such topics as *The American Civil War; Vampires: Legend, Literature and Film; Natural Life in the Finger Lakes Region;* and *Sondheim: Shaping Broadway in Our Times.*

Special children's programs include L'il Bears for children from 3 to 5 in a fully equipped Cornell preschool facility under trained early childhood specialists. Children between 5 and 8 can enjoy programs on geography, language, and food, with outings, games and crafts. Those between 9 and 12 choose among courses in printmaking, veterinary medicine, insects, cooking, and horse care among others. Teenagers have live-in counselors on hand to introduce them to college life, and choose from programs on acting, debate techniques, writing, and wilderness skills.

Everyone can take advantage of the recreational facilities on campus that include hiking trails, swimming pool, boating lake, tennis courts, golf, theater, concerts and cultural activities.

Price includes:
Accommodations, 16 meals, course tuition, parking fees, welcome and farewell parties, campus facilities, bus system.

Sample prices:
$715 adult, Donlon Hall, one week.
$385 teenager, $325 child 5 to 12, $250 toddlers, infants free.

Children:
Ages 3 to 16 welcome. Childcare for children younger than 3 available by special arrangement.

"First, we strive to give youngsters a taste of college life by combining learning activities with dorm living, campus recreation, and the opportunity to meet youngsters from many parts of the country. Second, we strive to give parents the comfort of pursuing their own interests while knowing that their children are nearby in responsible, caring hands."

CAU staff member.

Crow Canyon Archaeological Center
23390 County Road K
Cortez CO 81321
Phone: (303)565-8975/(800)422-8975
Fax: (303)565-4859
Contact: Lynn Dyer

Fascinated by archaeology? There's a unique center that provides research and field activities in southwestern Colorado. Its focus is piecing together information to understand the prehistoric people who once lived in the area and left behind the well-preserved stone ruins of the commuity that flourished there between 500 BC and 1300 AD.

The center offers an annual Family Week in August when adults and children can attend together. Depending on the ages of youngsters, they may help adults excavate in the field, work in the lab to analyze artifacts, take a trip to Mesa Verde National Park to see some of the largest cliff dwellings in the Southwest, and join in evening programs. Younger children participate in simulated excavation and lab activities. Families stay in the traditional log hogans on campus or in the lodge.

During the year, there are travel seminars and weeklong archaeological programs for adults, and student programs for school groups.

Price includes:
Accommodations, transportation after arrival in Cortez, all meals, excursions, instruction, entry fees, equipment.

Sample trips:
$775 adult, $425 child digging, $375 child non-digging, Family Week in August.
$775 adult, $550 student, one week, Excavation Program.

Children:
Minimum age accepted: 9. Best age: 9 to 18.
Students 14 and over may participate with their parents in any week-long excavation program offered, June to mid-October.

Denver Museum of Natural History
**2001 Colorado Boulevard
Denver CO 80205-5798
Phone: (303)370-6304
Contact: Pat Benn**

Special interest tours to a variety of places are offered every year by this outstanding museum. Led by local experts and staff members, the trips include places abroad as well as several in the United States.

Winter tours include an exploration of the wildlife and geology of Yellowstone National Park in winter, and a trip to the Amazon rainforest led by an expert on ecological anthropology, that focuses on the relationships between humans and their environment.

An exploration of Southeast Alaska includes kayaking, hiking and viewing the spectacular scenery from the observation deck of the *Wilderness Explorer*. An expedition to Mexico's Copper Canyon includes a tour of Chihuahua, a visit to a boarding school for the children of the Tarahumara Indians, and a train ride along the rim of the gorge.

Price includes:
Accommodations, transportation, meals, guides.
Sample trips:
$1,525 adult, 7 days, Yellowstone Winter Wildlife.
$1,525 adult, 9 days, Southeast Alaska.
$1,915 adult, 8 days, Copper Canyon, Mexico.
Children:
Welcome on some trips with parents.

Dillman's Creative Workshops
Dillman's Sand Lake Lodge
PO Box 98
Lac du Flambeau WI 54538
Phone: (715)588-3143/(800)359-2511
Contact: Sue Robertson

A beautiful setting by the 1,200-acre White Sand Lake and classes in watercolor painting, landscapes, seascapes and portrait painting, American Indian Studies, intaglio carving on gems and glass, calligraphy, nature photography, and more create an artistic vacation at this family lodge. From May to October, adults can join some 30 programs in the arts taught by enthusiasatic professionals. Family members can stay with students and pay a non-participant rate.

The Dillmans opened in 1935 planning to run a boys' camp. But no boys showed up. Instead families came to stay in the cabins, so they gave up the idea of a camp. Today, they are one of the most successful family vacation resorts. In 1990, readers of *Family Circle* magazine awarded the title of Best Cabin Resort in the country to the lodge.

The resort is situated on a 250-acre peninsula of northern Wisconsin surrounded by acres of woodlands. You can swim from two sandy beaches, practice golf, play tennis or volleyball, hike and bike through trails in the woods, canoe, kayak, water-ski and snorkel in the lake, or join guided nature hikes.

Price includes:
Tuition, room, breakfast and dinner, all facilities.
Sample prices:
$715 adult, Monday through Friday, Watercolor Creativity.
$625 adult, Tuesday through Saturday, Calligraphy.
$720 adult, Monday through Friday, Wearable Art/Scarves.
Student family: $494 per person, 6 days.
Children:
All ages welcome. 2 to 10, special rates available. No charge for under 2 years.

Dinosaur Discovery Expeditions
Dinamation
189-A Technology Drive
Irvine CA 92718
Phone: (714)753-9630/(800)547-0503
Fax: (714)753-9657
Contact: Vina Villanueva

Ever dreamed of going on an expedition to look for dinosaurs? This company offers you the chance to join a scientific team and discover how dinosaurs lived.

Under the direction of a qualified paleontologist, you look for and excavate fossils in the Morrison Formation of western Colorado, the high desert of Utah, and the high plains of Wyoming, to help solve the mysteries of the past. Expeditions set out weekly from May to September. You stay in hotels or lodges overnight.

In 1991, evidence of the earliest Nodosaur ever found in the western hemisphere was discovered. Another group found the world's largest and oldest Apatosaurus, and skulls from a Sauropod and an Allosaurus. An expedition in the Como Bluff area of Wyoming found bones from Allosaurs and Megalosaurs.

Dr. Robert T. Bakker, one of the paleontologists leading the Wyoming expeditions, said: "This is a rare chance to see fossil treasures in their natural context. Nothing can match the firsthand experience at a dinosaur quarry."

Price includes:
Accommodations, meals, transportation, materials, equipment, instruction.

Sample trips:
$695 adult, 5 days, Colorado Canyons Expedition.
$795 adult, 6 days, non-digging tour, Dinosaur Diamond Safari.
$850 adult, 7 days, Wyoming High Plains.

Children:
Minimum age, 13 years old, accompanied by a supervising adult.
July only: $525, 5 days, Kids Dino Camp, children 6 to 12, during Colorado Canyons Expedition.

DINOSAUR DAYS
"Though I've traveled the world and done a number of things that could be considered exotic and adventuresome, I've never had an experience to surpass my week in Grand Junction."
A visitor from Pennsylvania.

Grandtravel
6900 Wisconsin Avenue/Suite 706
Chevy Chase MD 20815
Phone: (301)986-0790/(800)247-7651
Contact: Helena T. Koenig

Specializing in vacation trips for grandparents and grandchildren, these travel programs have been developed by a team of teachers, psychologists, leisure counselors and educators. They're designed to be fun for older adults - including aunts, uncles, friends and surrogate grandparents - who want to share travel with children.

Helena T. Koenig, grandmother and founder of the travel agency of which Grandtravel is a division, believes traveling together is the best way for the generations to strengthen their relationship.

The company offers programs in the US and abroad, with a GrandTravel Escort accompanying travelers. In Washington DC, you visit the US Capitol, the Air and Space Museum, the Lincoln Memorial, Kennedy Center, the FBI building, the National Zoo, the White House, and tour Williamsburg and Annapolis. In New York City, you join a backstage tour of Radio City Music Hall, see the NBC TV studios, a baseball game, and take a breath-taking helicopter ride over the city. In California, there are visits to Universal City Studios, Disneyland, Santa Barbara, Solvang, Monterey and San Francisco.

Abroad, programs include a barge tour along the waterways of the Netherlands and Belgium, visits to the castles of England and Scotland, a safari in Kenya, and a tour of Australia among others.

Price includes:
Accommodations, transportation, most meals, snacks, guides, escorts, service charges, hotel taxes.

Sample trips:
$2,390 per person, one week, Washington DC.
$3,930 adult, $3,790 child, 15 days, England and Scotland.
$5,290 adult, $4,285 child 12 to 17, $3,940 child 7 to 11, 13 days, Barge Tour in Netherlands and Belgium.

Children:
All ages welcome, accompanied by grandparents.

"Don't change a thing! My granddaughter and I loved every minute of our tour to Holland. Looking forward to taking my grandson next year."
A grandparent.

A GUIDE FOR GRANDPARENTS AND GRANDCHILDREN

Before you leave on a trip together, it's a good idea to talk about what you expect and what you're used to. Here are a few questions to discuss.

What time do you go to bed?
Do you read in bed before you go to sleep?
Do you like a light on at night?
Do you get up early or prefer to sleep late?
Do you want a shower in the morning or at night?
Are you bringing a radio, hairdryer, camera?
What do you like to eat for breakfast?
What are your favorite foods?
What are you most interested in on this trip?
What do you NOT like doing?
What are you planning to pack?
What will the weather be like where we're going?
What kind of place are we going to stay?
What will we do in the evenings?

Parents may want to make sure children understand everyday rules of behavior: being quiet in museums and public places, not playing on elevators and escalators, picking up litter, saying where they're going, being on time, and remembering that grandparents are in charge.

Grandparents may find it helpful to find out about the places they're going to visit and be prepared to answer questions, plan some activities that will appeal to chldren, and dream up a few ideas for alternative activities if some things don't work out.

FAMILY TRAVEL

TIPI TOUR

"Each journey is an experience of the past, including a traditional tipi lifestyle and immersion in the history and customs of days gone by, and the present, through sharing daily life with young and old tribal members."

Robert Vetter.

Journeys Into American Indian Territory
PO Box 929
Westhampton Beach NY 11978
Phone: (516)878-8655/(800)458-2632
Fax: (516)878-8655
Contact: Robert Vetter

Anthropologist Robert Vetter studied at the University of Oklahoma and created this new unique program where visitors share an in-depth experience of the lives of modern Native Americans. The journeys are a weeklong adventure lead by Vetter and a staff of Indian people in Arizona and Oklahoma. Vetter began the program in 1988, assisted by Robert Fields "Boy Chief", a Pawnee Indian, and later with Michele Hummingbird (Cherokee) and Homer Buffalo (Kiowa-Comanche).

You join American Indians in Oklahoma, tour an Iowa tribal complex and have the chance to talk face-to-face at different settlements. You attend a performance of *The Trail of Tears* recounting the story of the forced migration of the Cherokee people from Georgia to the west, and participate in a fireside all-night ritual and a dance of the Eastern tribes. You also explore the Wichita Mountains, a ceremonial and spiritual center to the Plains Indians for hundreds of years, and visit the Indian Exposition, where 13 tribes are represented.

Price includes:
Accommodations, transportation, some meals, lectures, admission to all events.

Sample trips:
$795 per person, one week, *Bridging Two Worlds,* Oklahoma.
$895 per person, one week, *Native Sun I,* Arizona.

Children:
Any age welcome. Vetter likes to talk with families before they register. "This is an area of cultural sensitivity and in conversations over the phone I can explain what's involved," he said.

Smithsonian National Associate Program
1100 Jefferson Drive S.W.
Washington Dc 20560
Phone: (202)357-4700
Contact: Prudence Clendenning

The Smithsonian study tours cover almost every conceivable place and topic. More than 160 study tours and seminars are led by experts are offered year-round. The majority are designed for adults, but some accept children accompanied by parents or grandparents. All tours include seminars by outstanding experts as well as pre-trip information and reading lists. The emphasis is on learning about the places you visit and gaining a deeper understanding of your travels.

International tours study art history in Florence, photography in Paris, the symbols of faith in India and Nepal, Australia's Great Barrier Reef, the ecology of Panama, the Canadian Arctic, and China among others. You can also spend time in one place, living in Venice, Edinburgh, or Lhasa in Tibet.

Outdoor trips include whale-watching in Baja California, touring the Grand Canyon in Arizona, exploring the wonders of Florida's Everglades, or camping in Hawaii.

There are also cruises where you tour the rivers and waterways of Europe, cross the Atlantic on a tall sailing ship, or cruise along the coast of Maine on the *Nantucket Clipper* to see lighthouses and watch for gray whales and Atlantic puffins.

Price includes:
Airfare, accommodations, meals, sightseeing, tours, study leader, airport taxes, pre-trip notes, book packet, service charges, tips.
Sample trips:
$4,925 adult, 13 days, Splendors of Rome, Italy.
$5,875 adult, 16 days, Journey to the East, India and Nepal.
$6,465 adult, 16 days, Landscapes of the Yangtze River, China.
Children:
Suitable for older children. Anyone under 18 must be accompanied by a parent or guardian, and pay full price.

FAMILY DISCOVERY

"The expedition is participatory in nature, designed to appeal to children, their parents, and grandparents alike. It's an opportunity to discover this awesome part of America with your family."

Sven Olof-Lindblad.

Special Expeditions
720 Fifth Avenue
New York NY 10019
Phone: (212)765-7740/(800)762-0003
Fax: (212)265-3770
Contact: Sven-Olof Lindblad

A family trip that's been a success for 14 years takes you into the heart of the canyons and high desert scenery of the American Southwest. Leader Stewart Aitchison has photographed and written about the region for more than 25 years. He is still fascinated by its unique plants, animals, spectacular landscapes, and human history, and loves to explore it with visitors.

He leads groups of no more than 10 people to discover pioneer trails, swim and shoot the rapids in the San Juan river area, spend a day in Monument Valley, and join a llama trek where the llamas carry the gear through the woodlands around the canyons that have remains of ancient Anasazi culture. Highlights are seeing prehistoric Indian sites and meeting some of today's Navajos, Hopis, Utes, Mormons, cowboys and Indian traders.

"We have time to stop and identify a wildflower," he notes. "We can search for marine fossils left from an ancient sea; we can sit on the canyon's rim and be awe-struck by the fury of a distant thunderstorm, or filled with inspiration when the clouds part and a double rainbow spans a golden sandstone mesa."

Price includes:
Accommodations, transportation, meals, sightseeing, transfers, reading list, clothing list, phototographic hints.
Sample trips:
$2,750 adult, Canyons of Time, American Southwest.
Children:
Best age: 8 and over. Special approval needed for children under 8. All adults must be accompanied by a child.

ON THE WATER

Vacations on the water are a wonderful way to relax and unwind. Family boat trips are most enjoyable when children are old enough to swim, or at least know what to do if they happen to fall in the water.

WHAT'S A BOAT TRIP LIKE?

Different water provides very different vacaations. Renting a houseboat to explore a river is very different from riding a rubber raft down foaming whitewater. Paddling a canoe along the hundreds of miles of rivers in Minnesota's Boundary Waters is quite unlike a kayak trip in the turquoise waters of Baja. A sailboat trip exploring Florida's coastline is the polar opposite of sailing past the glaciers and whales of Alaska. For boat lovers, the choices depend on where you'd like to go and how active you want to be. Here are a few family experiences.

Houseboats Ahoy!

A leisurely slow-motion water experience is yours on a houseboat. Bob, Linda and their two children rent a six-person houseboat and chug around the inlets and open water of

Canada's St. Lawrence Islands National Park for a week every summer.

"We spend all our time in shorts or bathing suits. We fish and swim off the docks, or off the boat. You can even dive from the top deck of the boat if you're sure the water is deep enough. The river is vast. A trip all the way across the St. Lawrence Seaway, dodging 10-story-high freighters, to Heart Island to check in at US Customs if you go ashore in the US, is a thrill not to be missed. We've learned to move from one island to another early in the day because the docks fill up, and we look for smaller docks because they're quieter."

Meals are carefully planned. Frozen casseroles and sauces are kept in one cooler, and drinks and ice in another.

River Rafting Thrills

For excitement riding the rapids down the rivers of the West, take a rafting vacation. Patsy and John went with their two children, aged 10 and 12, and enthused: "Though it's months later, we still talk about shooting the white water of Rattlesnake Canyon, floating in the river's current, and sleeping on the sand under the stars. We chose a four-day trip on Utah's Green River, because it offered medium rapids, miles of spectacular scenery, and hikes to see ancient petroglyphs on canyon walls. From Grand Junction, a small plane took us over barren, mountainous canyon landscape to Sand Wash where we met our guides and saw our first rubber rafts. After a safety talk, we put on lifejackets, took off our watches, and paddled off."

The first day was smooth with only riffles on the water, and they camped at night on the beach, learning to put up the tents. Meals included chicken, spaghetti, steak, pasta, plus cake, cookies and ice cream for dessert, and coffee, tea, and fruit

GRANDPARENTS TOO

"On our trip, a grandfather brought along his two grandchildren, aged 12 and 14. He told us he'd taken his own children rafting every summer, and now he was starting again. It was the first time they had ever been rafting and they loved it."

Woman on Yampa River trip.

juices. As the fire died down, people drifted off to climb into sleeping bags, and an enormous full moon slowly rose over the canyon walls, bathing the river and trees in silver.

"The next day we could hear the sound of the rapids breaking on the rocks way before we see it. There was plenty of time to find a place on the raft to sit and a rope to hold on to. In the rapids we bounced over the waves, and got splashed - or drenched - by the spray and waves. It was exciting and fun."

Paddle Your Own Canoe

A more peaceful water trip is to take a canoe along quieter waterways, in the Minnesota boundary waters on the Canada-US border. The rhythm of a canoe vacation is like river-rafting. You adjust to your boat, paddle down the river, camp out at designated sites on the shore, enjoy a delicious camp meal around the fire, and relax under the stars. The next day you pack your gear, reload the canoe, and take off to paddle down the river again. There may be rough water in some stretches, and you might have to portage the canoe along the shore if there's a difficult patch of river water. There's often time for hikes and excursions inland, and you may see elk and deer, or catch some fresh fish.

Kayak With The Whales

A kayak is a lightweight craft for one or two people that's ideal for ocean or river exploration. Some kayakers enjoy riding rivers and whitewater rapids; others prefer to bounce over the waves on the sea. In Mexico's Baja California, you can paddle a 20-foot kayak close to the gray whales on their annual migration to the warm bay waters. Even novices can kayak.

One paddler noted: "Some simple instruction about leaning into the wave and paddling cross-wave got our group of mostly

LANDLUBBERS' LIST

Wet suit. Ask if you need one.
Wet suit booties. Keep your feet warm.
Pair jeans
Jogging suit
2 shirts, long sleeved
Sweater
3 T-shirts
Bathing suit
Pair shorts
Hat with string
2 pairs tennis shoes
Flip-flops or sandals
Warm jacket
Pair mittens or gloves
Underwear
2 pairs long underwear.
2 pairs socks.
Rainjacket and pants
Sunscreen
Hand lotion
Soap
Shampoo
Toilet paper.
Towel
Water bottle
Flashlight
Fishing equipment
Camera
Ziplock bags.

novices quickly into the swing of the sport. Each day we paddled a few hours at our own pace southward through the usually placid bay, coming ashore in early afternoon to set up our tents and eat lunch. In the afternoons we were free to paddle around on our own or hike across the island to see whale bones, pelican skulls and shells.

"In the late afternoon we'd paddle out to look for whales. We saw one within 20 feet of us standing on its head for three minutes, its tail sticking straight up in the air. Once a baby whale came so close to one of the boats that you could touch its head. We came back to camp just in time for dinner, and then sat around a giant bonfire talking about the day's whale sightings - and ourselves. Though daytime temperatures were in the 80s, evenings were quite cold. I was glad I had brought my down jacket and gloves."

PREPARATIONS

Renting a houseboat or traveling on a group tour means that almost everything is provided. You need only bring personal items. On most boat trips, the less you have, the better. There's never a lot of extra room aboard. You may need a wetsuit in spring or early summer because the weather and water can be chilly. In July and August it's usually warmer.

WITH CHILDREN

Babies and Toddlers: Usually, children under 6 are too young for most boat trips, unless they're good swimmers and parents feel comfortable with them in deep water.

Youngsters and Teenagers: Children over 6 are ideal boat passengers. They like the adventure and obey safety procedures, and respond to the freedom of river life.

BE PREPARED

Things can go wrong on boat trips. One important rule is to make sure everyone wears a life jacket at all times, and that it's securely fastened. If someone falls in the water, at least the life jacket will keep him or her afloat. Listen carefully to safety rules, and make sure everyone in the family obeys them, and knows what to do in an emergency.

Another factor to consider that there are often long periods of paddling, or waiting when things go wrong while a course of action is decided. It may be hard for children to understand about sitting quietly. On one trip, the boat wedged itself between two rocks. It took a couple of hours to rig up a rope to ease it back into the water. Everyone had to climb out and wait on the rocks above the rushing river water. You should be sure that your children are old enough to cope in unexpected emergencies and will obey instructions.

Should there be a serious accident, most boatmen have radio emergency contact with the outside world, and can call for assistance.

RESOURCE GUIDE TO VACATIONS ON THE WATER

Adventure Bound
2932 H Road
Grand Junction CO 81505
Phone: (303)241-5633/(800)423-4668
Fax: (303)241-5633
Contact: Tom Kleinschnitz

This company leads river-rafting trips by oar, paddle, large pontoon, inflatable kayak or combinations, so that there's plenty of room for variety. Its staff are experienced and professional guides, with excellent experience in river running and are well informed about the geology and history of the Colorado Plateau.

Trips explore Desolation and Grey Canyons in the Green River Wilderness, Lodore and Yampa Rivers in Dinosaur National Monument, and Westwater, Ruby and Horsethief Canyons on the Colorado River. Here you float past red sandstone cliffs to the area of black rocks, the oldest exposed rock in Utah, and may spot bald eagles, golden eagles, hawks, falcons and vultures. There's also a trip through Cataract Canyon with some of the wildest whitewater in America.

Price includes:
Camping accommodations, all meals on the river, safety equipment, transportation to put in point and return to hotel, guides.
Sample trips:
$460 adult, $425 child, 4 days, Yampa River, Colorado.
$460 adult, $425 child, 4 days, Green River Wilderness, Utah.
$550 adult, $505 child, 5 days, Cataract Canyon, Colorado.
Children:
"We welcome families," says Tom Kleinschnitz. "The water depends on the time of year, and we usually recommend Lodore Canyon and the Green River in July and August for younger children, if they can handle the activity on the boat - sometimes that's too much for them. Parents can call me to ask about trips because everything depends on the child."

OVERBOARD

"Our son, who's 11 and a good swimmer, was knocked off the raft by a wave. I watched as he did exactly as we'd been told, paddling and facing forward, feet up, until he was hauled into the boat by the guide. Then he scrambled back to his place to go on paddling. I was terrified but he thought it was exciting because he knew what to do."

Parent on river trip.

Alaska Wilderness Sailing Safaris
PO Box 1313
Valdez AK 99686
Phone: (907)835-5175
Fax: (907)835-4836
Contact: Nancy Lethcoe

Naturalist guided sailing and kayaking trips in Alaska's Prince William Sound are the speciality of this company. Drs. Jim and Nancy Lethcoe have lived aboard and sailed in Alaskan waters for the past 22 years. They are the authors of *Cruising Guide to Prince William Sound*, and other books on the region.

Trips begin in Valdez, which is 360 miles by car from Anchorage, a drive through historic farmland and spectacular scenery. Sailing boats leave Growler Island Wilderness Camp and all trips include hiking, kayaking and dinghy trips to explore the coastline.

You spot river otters, sea otters, seals, eagles and shore and sea birds. You observe puffins, black bears, and the fascinating geology of the region. You see an advancing tidewater glacier knocking down trees. The area is surrounded by snow-covered peaks and glaciers that descend to sea level.

Trips range from 3 to 7 days, and are led by a qualified navigator and guide. All sailboats are equipped with heaters, full galleys and comfortable berths. Experienced sailors can skipper their own boat and provide their own food.

Price includes:
Accommodations, transportation, all meals, guides, instruction, equipment, pre-trip orientation, insurance.
Sample trips:
$450, 3 days, guided trip, Sea Otters & Glaciers.
$1,250, 6 days, guided trip, Whale Watching & Glaciers.
$700, 6 days, experienced sailors, 30-foot sailboat.
Children:
12 and under half price. Minimum age: 3 months.
Best age: 6 years and older.

PEACE ON THE WATER
"We believe that the silence of our flotilla of sailing vessels supplemented by our fleet of stable, inflatable sea kayaks provide the perfect means of unobtrusively exploring this still unspoiled wilderness."

Nancy Lethcoe.

American River Touring Association
**Star Route 73
Groveland CA 95321
Phone: (209)962-7873/(800)323-2782
Contact: Eric White**

ARTA is a non-profit corporation, founded in 1963, which aims to run enjoyable river trips in the West and bring a unique blend of enthusiasm, curiousity and spirit to them.

"We feel that the nation's wild rivers should not be exploited for individual gain, and our philosophy ensures that any surplus revenues generated by our trips are reinvested in the company or donated to conservation organizations," notes Eric White.

You can select from a variety of family trips on the Rogue and North Umpqua rivers in Oregon, the Green river through Lodore and Desolation canyons in Utah, Colorado and Arizona, and the Salmon river in Idaho. There's a choice of oar raft, paddle raft, oar and paddle combination raft, or an inflatable canoe. A staff member notes: "On some days we may designate a kid's boat, or have a no-talent show, or an Un-Birthday Party, and on other days we may do all three. The only guarantee is that we will have fun."

The company also offers whitewater workshops, where you learn about wilderness river touring, and a Professional Guide Training Workshop for people interested in working as commercial guides.

Price includes:
Accommodations, transportation, equipment, all meals, guides, instruction, excursions, pre-trip orientation. Special Family Trips allow an additional 15% off the regular youth rate for each youth accompanied by an adult.

Sample trips:
$330 adult, $275 youth, 3 days, North Umpqua, Oregon.
$440 adult, $370 youth, 4 days, Green/Lodore Canyon, Colorado.
$1,460 adult, $1,260 youth, 12 day, Salmon River, Idaho.

Children:
All ages welcome.

"We had a truly great experience. We paddled the rapids, saw the scenery, smelled the smells, swam, hiked, did the water slide into a mountain pool, and met some terrific people."
Participant on Rogue River trip.

"The scenery was fantastic, the food was excellent, the guides were friendly hardworking, helpful, funny, witty and very informative."
Participant on Yampa River trip.

Baja Expeditions
**2625 Garnet Avenue
San Diego CA 92109
Phone: (619)581-3311/(800)843-6967
Contact: Director**

Baja Expeditions is Mexico's largest and oldest outfitter of adventure travel in the Baja area. Since 1974, they've been exploring the territory and discovering its secrets. They offer a variety of boat trips to watch whales, dolphins and sea lions as well as to scuba dive, snorkel, kayak and sail in the Sea of Cortez.

In winter the whales migrate to the waters of Baja, and congregate in the same places every year. A 4-day whale-watching special excursion explores Magdalena Bay with superb views of whales at close range from the boat and from skiffs. You live aboard the *Don Jose,* a 16-passenger motor vessel, and take skiffs for trips to a narrow mangrove estuary teeming with fish and birds including herons, egrets and osprey.

A longer cruise travels the length of the Sea of Cortez, and visits many of the islands John Steinbeck saw on the voyage he described in *The Log of the Sea of Cortez*. You see whales, dolphins, sea lions, sea birds, as well as brown pelicans, terns, gulls, and blue-footed boobies.

For the independent spirit, the company offers sea kayaks with a rudder, and you can paddle from beach to beach around Espiritu Santo Island. The island has wonderful beaches, deep canyons, a fresh water well, and superb waters for snorkeling. You can also join a trip to sea kayak along the coat of Costa Rica.

Price includes:
Airfare from Los Angeles to La Paz, land arrangements, meals, accommodations, beverages, hotels, most trip-related equipment.
Sample trips:
$550 adult, 4 days, Whale Watching Special, Don Jose.
$1,300 adult, 9 days, Sea Kayaking, Espiritu Santo Island.
$2,295 adult, 10 days, Steinbeck Journey aboard Don Jose.
Children:
Minimum age: 8, but varies with trips. Children pay full price.

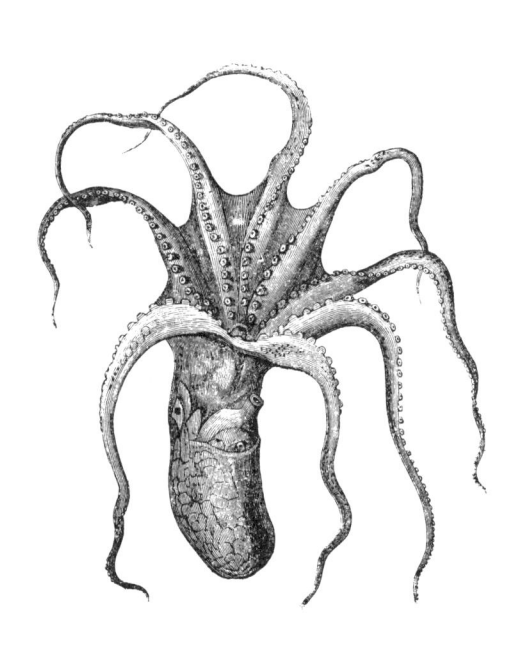

Canoe Country Escapes
194 South Franklin Street
Denver CO 80209
Phone: (303)722-6482
Contact: Brooke & Eric Durland

Exploring the Northwoods of the Minnesota-Ontario Boundary Waters is the specialty of this company, which for 15 years has led canoe expeditions into the thousands of square miles of lakes and forests once home to the Ojibway Indians.

They offer wilderness experiences with a guide where you paddle, portage, follow a route French-Canadian trappers once used, camp, swim and fish. You can choose an Escape Trip and canoe deep into the heart of the Boundary Waters Canoe Area Wilderness. Or try a softer lodge-to-lodge trip where you paddle during the day and stay in bed-and-breakfasts, inns, and lakeside lodges.

Four Family Trips are available. The schedule avoids hard days of paddling, includes a layover day every other day, and has plenty of great swimming and fishing. What's more, youngsters prove to be excellent naturalists and spot frogs, mushrooms, blueberries, spider webs, and moose droppings that adults often miss.

The company can also arrange custom guided trips for families or groups who cannot come on scheduled dates.

Price includes:
Accommodations, transportation, all meals, guides, instruction. Equipment available for rental.
Sample trips:
$272 each, 3 people, 2 days, custom guided trip, canoe and camp.
$535 adult, $360 children under 12, 5 days, canoe and camp.
$695 adult, 5 days, Lodge to Lodge canoeing.
Children:
5 and up welcome. Best age: Over 8.

Gunflint Northwoods Outfitters
Gunflint Lodge
750 Gunflint Trail
Grand Marais MN 55604
Phone: (800)362-5251
Fax: (218)388-9429
Contact: Sheryl Hinderman

The Kerfoot family are experts in trips in the Boundary Waters Canoe Area Wilderness. The company emphasizes a policy of Minimum Impact, which encourages the preservation of wilderness.

Their Guided Family Trip, limited to nine people, is designed to give children a chance to learn wilderness skills including firebuilding, camp cooking, canoeing, and fishing as well as bird-watching and moose finding.

On the weeklong Lodge to Lodge Canoe Trip your luggage is portaged to pre-set campsites, and you paddle with only your personal gear. A more challenging trip is the Adventure Week program, which explores the wilder areas of the region. The company also offers self-guided canoe trip packages.

You can explore the area and stay at Gunflint Lodge, open year-round. There's a resident fishing pro to lead trips, often booked up a year in advance, and fishing guides to show you to the best spots. You can rent a boat, join two naturalists on hikes and raft trips during the summer months, and sign up for special biker and hiker weeks.

Price includes:
Accommodations, all meals, activities, guides.
Sample costs:
$535 adult, $360 child, 6-night, canoe package.
$1,695 to $2,195 up to 4 people in lodge, 7-night family package.
Children:
Canoe trips: Children welcome with adults.
At the Lodge: Under 4; babysitting available.
5 to 16: Wilderness activities, cookouts, wilderness skills.

Houseboat Holidays Ltd.
RR 3 Gananoque
Ontario K7G 2V5, Canada
Phone: (613)382-2842
Contact: Dev Nicholl-Carne

Dev Nicholl-Carne is happy to rent you a houseboat to explore the 50 miles of the St. Lawrence River and the Thousand Islands. He's been in business since 1973, and asserts: "We may not be the largest houseboat operator in Canada, but we are determined to remain the best."

You don't need previous boating experience because full handling and docking instructions are provided. Docking and anchoring space at the Canadian Park Islands is free. On the major islands, you'll find interpretive programs and hiking trails to introduce you to the wide variety of plant and animal life in the area.

All houseboats meet government safety regulations, and are equipped with navigation lights, life jackets, horn, 2 anchors, fire extinguisher, flares, and first aid kit. There's a covered forward deck, a rooftop sundeck, hot and cold running water, shower, propane stove with oven, refrigerator, cabin heater, bedding, galley, and flush toilet.

You will be provided with specially marked marine charts showing points of interest, docking and shopping facilities.

Price includes:
Fully equipped houseboat, dockage at Canadian National Park Islands, sheets, pillows and blankets, propane, on-site parking.
Sample prices (in Canadian $$):
$750, Brown Model, one week from May 28 to June 25.
$900, Red Model, one week from August 20 to Sept. 17.
$1,150, Blue Model, one week from June 25 to August 20.
Weekend and mid-week rates range from $425 to $700.
Children:
All ages welcome.

HOUSEBOAT HAUNTS
"Each island is unique. You can go from one to another, or stay for several days at your favorite. We love to find new places."
Family on houseboat trip.

Marine Sciences Under Sail
PO Box 3994
Hollywood FL 33023
Phone: (305)983-9015
Contact: JoAnn Bowie

Hands-on, get-wet adventures in small boats that take families on trips to discover the life and history of the sea around Florida are offered by this non-profit organization. Marine Sciences Under Sail leaders want to show people the vital role the sea and coastal zone play in their lives and the necessity for protecting these natural resources.

Hundreds of small boats once sailed the Florida waters among the mangrove islands, skimming across the shallows, skirting the turquoise ripples of the coral reefs, and paddling among the Everglades of the peninsula, but few remain today.

You can take a trip for a day, a week, or a couple of weeks. There's plenty of time to snorkel in the clear water and to observe coral reefs, turtle grass and mangrove creeks just as those on sailboats did a hundred years ago. However, this isn't a luxury cruise; living aboard a small boat is more like camping in a tent. You bring your own food and drink and adjust to the lack of space.

Price includes:
Accommodations only. You bring food and drink.
Sample trips:
$33 each person, 6 people, daytime sailing trip.
$38 each person, 6 people, overnight sail.
$95 each person, 2 people, overnight sail.
Children:
Accepted at any age. School groups welcome.

CAPTAIN'S ADVICE
"The ocean is our bathtub, sea water toothbrushing is a distinct shock for the usual oral biota, and you may choose to sleep topside under the stars."

FAMILY TRAVEL

GRAND CANYON THRILLS
"We had a great trip. The outstanding feature was the guides. Their experience, knowledge, patience and amicable disposition allowed my children and I—true city slickers—to really feel the majesty of the Grand Canyon."
Family from Illinois.

O.A.R.S.
PO Box 67
Angels Camp CA 95222
Phone: (209)736-4677/(800)346-6277
Fax: (209)736-2902
Contact: Kay Metherell

"To go rafting with your family is to share with them the adventure of a lifetime," notes an O.A.R.S. staff person. "The exhilaration and thrill of challenging and conquering a rapid, the excitement of camping under the stars, the scenery of the American West, has made river running the vacation of choice for many of today's active families."

O.A.R.S. stands for Outdoor Adventure River Specialists, and the company was founded 25 years ago by George Wendt. Today, past passengers are signing up for trips with their young children. The company has a special Family Discount Policy; two members pay full price, and everyone else in the family gets a 15% discount, no matter how large the group.

Recommended family trips include the San Juan River, in Utah, where the rapids are mild and the sunsets spectacular. In Wyoming, an easy trip in the Grand Tetons paddles along the shores of Jackson Lake and floats down the Snake River, where you may see elk, deer, moose and even buffalo.

Oregon's Rogue River is one of the original Wild and Scenic rivers in the national river protection network, and and the raft trips winds its way amid the trees and greenery of Siskiyou national Forest, where you'll find fishing holes and swimming pools in fern grottoes.

Price includes:
Accommodations, transportation, all meals, equipment, guides, instruction, entry fees, pre-trip orientation.
Sample trips:
$245 adult, $227 children over 4, 2 days, Grand Tetons, Wyoming.
$656 adult, $600 children over 7, 5 days, Rogue River, Oregon.
$570 adult, $520 children over 7, 4 days, Lower Salmon, Idaho.
Children:
Minimum age accepted: 4. Best age: 7 and older.

Rocky Mountain River Tours
PO Box 520
Eagle ID 83616
Phone: (208)345-2400
Contact: Dave Mills

Dave and his wife Sheila first offered raft trips on the Middle Fork in 1978, riding through 105 miles of the most primitive country in the world - wild, untamed, and still relatively untouched. You travel in oar rafts, paddle boats and inflatable kayaks, with one guide for every four guests. Along the way you gaze at pine forests and canyon cliffs, hike to Indian sites, remnants of the Tukudeka mountain tribe, and see pictographs in an Indian cave. There are abandoned mines, old grave markers, and time for fishing, bird-watching and swimming.

At night, you camp on white sand beaches, near hot springs, shaded by tall conifers. Sheila is an expert Dutch oven cook, and her book, *Rocky Mountain Kettle Cuisine*, now in its second edition, includes Avocado Frittata, Ginger Marinated Roast Breast of Duck with Cherry Chutney, and Yogurt Chocolate Cake.

"We offer wilderness trips on the Middle Fork of the Salmon River for all ages, with everything supplied but your toothbrush and your smiles," says Dave Mills. "Small kids have the best time during July and August when the water is warm enough for swimming."

The company won a 1992 Idaho Governor's Conference on Recreation and Tourism Award "for their efforts to provide a quality whitewater rafting experience while preserving Idaho's environment."

Price includes:
Accommodations, equipment, transportation, all meals, excursions, guides, instruction, entry fees, pre-trip orientation, insurance.

Sample trips:
$775, 4 days, May and June.
$950, 5 days, August and September.
$1,195, 6 days, all summer.
Children under 15, 10% discount.

Children:
Minimum age accepted: 6.

"Our family vote was unanimous—never have we enjoyed such a wonderful vacation. Dick probably traveled 75% of the river in a kayak. Our Middle Fork memories are preserved in our kids journals and three hundred pictures."
Family from Boston.

"It was an unmatchable adventure. We loved it. We liked the short river days - we swam and hiked and kayaked from camp."
Family from Illinois.

Western River Expeditions
7258 Racquet Club Drive
Salt Lake City UT 84121
Phone: (801)942-6669/(800)453-7450
Fax: (801)942-8514
Contact: Larry Lake, President

For more than 30 years, this company has taken guests through some of the most spectacular scenery in the world on rafting trips on the Green River, Colorado River, and Idaho's Salmon River. Most trips are in large power-driven rubber rafts, though some are oar-powered, or paddle boats, where you paddle the raft with a crew.

"For a first time river experience, I recommend a 4-day trip on Utah's Green River," says Larry Lake, president. "With more than 60 rapids, there is plenty of white-water adventure, but stretches of calm water offer a perfect change of pace."

For bigger thrills, try the 50-mile Westwater Canyon on the upper Colorado, or the exploding white water of Cataract Canyon in Canyonlands National Park.

There is also a 6-day trip through the Grand Canyon, where you'll gaze up at vast canyon cliffs and ride through wild rapids, hike to Anasazi Indian sites, shower in waterfalls, and share evening stories around a campfire on the beach.

Price includes:
Accommodations, transportation to and from the river, all meals, boats, guides.
Sample trips:
$665 adult, $332.50 youth 7 to17, 4 days, Green River, Utah.
$855 adult, $527 youth 7 to17, 6 days, Salmon River, Idaho.
$1,265, 6 days, Grand Canyon, Colorado River.
Children:
Accompanied by parent or responsible adult. Some trips are limited to children over 12. Most accept children 7 and over.

Whitewater Challengers
PO Box 8
White Haven PA 18661
Phone: (717)443-9532
Contact: Director

There's river-rafting on the east coast too. Summer white-water raft trips on the Lehigh River in Pennsylvania are an easy way to get introduced to river-rafting. For more challenging rapids, they'll take you to the Hudson River Gorge, a remote wilderness experience in New York's Adirondack State Park, and the Moose River. The company also offers a weekend white-water kayak school with instruction in paddling techniques.

Price includes:
Instruction, equipment, guides.
Sample trips:
$29 adult, $19 children under 17, one day, Lehigh River.
$75 adult and children over 16, weekend, Hudson River Gorge.
Children:
Minimum age accepted: 5 on Lehigh River.

Zoar Outdoor
Mohawk Trail
Charlemont MA 01339
Phone: (413)339-4010/(800)532-7483
Fax: (413)337-8436
Contact: Bruce Lessels

Outdoor adventure programs with instruction in canoeing, kayaking and rafting are offered by this company in the Berkshires. There's also a special racing clinic for intermediate and advanced paddlers.

For families, there are one-day rafting trips on the Zoar Gap and weekend programs of rafting and kayaking on the Deerfield River.

Price includes:
Transportation, some meals, excursions, guides, instruction, equipment, pre-trip orientation, insurance.
Sample trip:
$59 adult, $44 children, one day white-water rafting.
Children:
Minimum age accepted: 7. Best age: Over 7.

BIBLIOGRAPHY

RECOMMENDED PUBLICATIONS.

Barker, Gayle & Pinick, Joanna. *Great Resorts for Parents and Kids. A Travel Guide to US Resorts.* (Editor's Ink, Seattle, WA).

Butler, Arlene Kay. *Traveling with Children & Enjoying It.* (Globe Pequot, Chester, CT).

Cleaver, Joanne. *Doing Children's Museums: A Guide to 265 Hands-On Museums.* (Williamson).

Cochran, Barbara Ann & Cochran Kelly, Lindy. *Teach Your Child to Ski.* (Stephen Greene Press/Pelham Books, NY).

Dickerman, Pat. *Farm, Ranch & Country Vacations.* (Adventure Guides, New York, NY).

Eagle Walking Turtle. *Indian America: A Traveler's Companion.* (John Muir, Santa Fe, NM).

Frome, Michael. *National Park Guide.* (Prentice Hall, Englewood Cliffs, NJ)

Frommer, Arthur. *New World of Travel.* (Prentice Hall, Englewood Cliffs, NJ)

Greenspan, Rick & Kahn, Hal. *The Camper's Companion: the pack-along guide for better outdoor trips.* (Foghorn Press, San Francisco, CA).

Jordon, Dorothy & Cohen, Marjorie. *Great Vacations With Your Kids.* (E. P. Dutton, New York, NY).

Jordon, Dorothy. *Family Travel Times Newsletter.* 10 issues a year. (FTT, 45 W.18th St., 7th flr. Tower, New York, NY 10011).

Kaye, Evelyn. *Eco-Vacations: Enjoy Yourself and Save the Earth.* (Blue Penguin Publications, Boulder, CO).

Kaye, Evelyn. *Travel and Learn: The New Guide to Educational Travel.* (Blue Penguin Publications, Boulder, CO).

Kilgore, Eugene. *Ranch Vacations: The Complete Guide to Guest and Resort, Fly-fishing and Cross-country Skiing Ranches.* (John Muir, Santa Fe, NM).

Kimbrough, John. *The Vacation Home Exchange & Hospitality Guide.* (Kimco Communications, Fresno CA).

Lansky, Vicki. *Trouble-Free Travel with Children.* (The Book Peddlers, CA).

Martin, Bob. *Fly There For Less: How to Slash the Cost of Air Travel Worldwide.* (Teak Wood Press, Kissimmee, FL).

McMillon, Bill. *Volunteer Vacations: A Directory of Short-Term Adventures that will benefit you and others.* (Chicago Review Press, Chicago, IL).

Meyers, Carole Terwilliger. *Miles of Smiles: 101 Great Car Games & Activities.* (Carousel Press, Albany, CA).

Meyers, Carole Terwilliger. *Family Travel Guides Catalogue.* (PO Box 6061, Albany, CA 94706).

Murphy, Laura & Michael. *A Traveler's Guide to Vacation Rentals in Europe.* (E. P. Dutton, New York, NY).

Read, Margery & Will, Richard. *Dinosaur Digs: A Guide to Parks and Museums where you can discover Prehistoric Creatures.* (Country Roads Press, Boston, MA).

Showker, Kay. *Caribbean Ports of Call: A Guide for Today's Cruise Passenger.* (Globe Pequot, Chester, CT).

Silverman, Goldie. *Backpacking with Babies and Small Children.* (Wilderness Press, CA).

Torrens, Diane. *Fielding's Family Vacations USA.* (Fielding Travel Books/Morrow, New York, NY).

Travel Guides Series: *Birnbaum, Fodor, Frommer,* and other general guides have information about traveling with children. Fodor has a guide to *Skiing in the USA and Canada* with good information about children's activity programs. Also publisher John Muir's *Kidding Around* series provides short illustrated guidebooks to several cities for young travelers.

Walter, Claire. *Rocky Mountain Skiing.* (Fulcrum, Boulder, CO).

Wheeler, Maureen. *Travel With Children: A Survival Kit for Travel in Asia.* (Lonely Planet, Berkeley, CA).

188 *FAMILY TRAVEL*

RESOURCE DIRECTORY

VACATIONS FOR BABIES AND TODDLERS

American Wilderness Experience
ASPIRE
Beds Abroad
Bluffdale Vacation Farm
Chatauqua Institution
Cheyenne River Ranch
Colorado 40 DGRA Ranches
Colorado Dude & Guest Ranch Association
Cornell's Adult University
Dude Ranchers Association
FamilyHostel
Grandtravel
Gunflint Northwds Outfitters
Harvey's Mt. View Inn
High Island Guest Ranch
House Exchange Program
Houseboat Holidays
Ingeberg Acres
Inn at East Hill Farm
Interhome
Intervac US
Israel Kibbutz Hotels
Michel Farm Vacations
Mountain Dale Farm
Olde Fogie Farm
Overseas Adventure Travel
Rascals in Paradise
Rocky Mtn. Cattle Moovers
Sierra Club
Smithsonian
Vacation Exchange Club
Villas & Apartments Abroad
Wilderness Trails Ranch
Wildland Adventures
Yellowstone National Park
Zoetic Research

VACATIONS FOR AGES 5 TO 12

Adventure Bound
Alaska Wildland
Alaska Wilderness Sailing Safaris
American River Touring Assn.
American Wilderness Experience
ASPIRE
Baja Expeditions
Beds Abroad
Big Five Tours & Expeditions
Bluffdale Vacation Farm
Campbell Folk School
Canoe Country Escapes
Chatauqua Institution
Cheyenne River Ranch
Colorado Dude & Guest Ranch Association
Copper Mountain skiing
Cornell's Adult University
Country Inns Along the Trail
Craftsbury Nordic Center
Crested Butte skiing
Crow Canyon Archaeological Ctr.
Denver Museum of Natural History
Diamond Peak skiing
Dillmans Creative Workshops
Dinosaur Discovery
Dude Ranchers Association
Ecotour Expeditions
FamilyHostel
Grand Targhee
Grandtravel
Gunflint Northwoods Outfitters
Harvey's Mt. View Inn
High Island Guest Ranch
House Exchange Program
House Exchange Program
Houseboat Holidays
Ingeberg Acres
Inn at East Hill Farm
Interhome
Intervac US
Israel Kibbutz Hotels
Journeys into American Indian Territory
Marine Sciences Under Sail
Michel Farm Vacations
Montecito-Sequoia Nordic Ski Resort
Mountain Dale Farm
National Wildlife Federation
OARS
Okeanos Ocean Research Fndn.
Olde Fogie Farm
Olympic Park Institute
Overseas Adventure Travel
Pacific Northwest Field Seminars
Purgatory/Durango skiing
Rascals in Paradise
Rocky Mountain Cattle Moovers
Rocky Mountain Nature Assoc.
Rocky Mountain River Tours
Russian Homestay
Schweitzer skiing
Sierra Club
Snowbird skiing
Special Expeditions
Steamboat skiing
Stowe Mountain Resort
Sun Valley skiing
Tandem Touring Company
Untours Idyll
Vacation Exchange Club
Villas & Apartments Abroad
Waterville Valley skiing
Western River Expeditions
White Mountains skiing
Whitewater Challengers
Wilderness Trails Ranch
Wildland Adventures
Yellowstone Institute
Yellowstone National Park
Zoar Outdoor
Zoetic Research

VACATIONS FOR TEENAGERS

Adirondack Mountain Club
Adventure Bound
Alaska Wilderness Sailing Safaris
Alaska Wildland
American Wilderness Experience
American Hiking Society
American Inst. for Foreign Study
American River Touring Assoc.
Appalachian Mountain Club
Avenir Adventures
Backroads
Baja Expeditions
Big Five Tours & Expeditions
Canoe Country Escapes
Chatauqua Institution
Cheyenne River Ranch
Colorado Dude & Guest Ranch Association
Copper Mountain
Craftsbury Nordic Center
Crested Butte skiing
Crow Canyon Archaeological Ctr.
Denver Museum of Natural History
Diamond Peak skiing

Dinosaur Discovery
Dude Ranchers Association
Ecotour Expeditions
FamilyHostel
Forum Travel International
Grand Targhee skiing
Grandtravel
Gunflint Northwoods Outfitters
High Island Guest Ranch
Hostelling International
Houseboat Holidays
Israel Kibbutz Hotels
Journeys
Marine Sciences Under Sail
Mobility International
Montecito-Sequoia Nordic Ski Resort
Myths and Mountains
National Wildlife Federation
National and State Parks
North Carolina National Forests
OARS
Okeanos Ocean Research Fndn.
Olympic Park Institute
Overseas Adventure Travel
Pacific Northwest Field Seminars
Pocono Environmental Ed. Center
Purgatory/Durango skiing
Rascals in Paradise
Roads Less Traveled
Rocky Mountain Cattle Moovers
Rocky Mountain Nature Assoc.
Rocky Mountain River Tours
Russian Homestay
Schweitzer skiing
Sierra Club
Smithsonian
Snowbird skiing

Special Expeditions
Steamboat skiing
Stowe Mountain Resort
Sun Valley skiing
Tandem Touring Company
USDA Forest Service
Volunteers for Peace
Waterville Valley skiing
Western River Expeditions
White Mountains skiing
Whitewater Challengers
Wilderness Trails Ranch
Wildland Adventures
World Learning
Yellowstone Institute
Yellowstone National Park
Vermont State Parks
Zoar Outdoor
Zoetic Research

CAMPING DIRECTORY

**US Govt. Printing Office
Supt. of Documents
Washington DC
   20402-3925.
Phone: (800)452-1111.**
Send $4 for a National Park Service Camping Guide, Stock Number 024-005-01080-7, listing park campgrounds.

Regional offices:
National Park Service
PO Box 158
Bowie AZ 85605

National Park Service
4202 Alhambra Avenue
Martinez CA 94553

National Park Service
Rocky Mountain Region
12795 W Alameda Parkway
Denver CO 80225

National Park Service
PO Box 666
Grand Marais MN 55604

National Park Service
PO Box 40
Capulin NM 88414

National Park Service
3501 Old Nashville Highway
Murfreesboro TN 37129

National Park Service
Pacific NW Regional office
83 S King Street/Suite 212
Seattle WA 98104

**Bureau of Land Mgmt.
1849 C Street NW
Room 5600
Washington DC 20240**
Ask for a list of BLM campsites.

**Department of the Army/
USACE
Regional Brochures, IM-MV-N
3909 Halls Ferry Road
Vicksburg MS 39180-6199**
Ask for list of USACE campsites.

**US Fish & Wildlife Service
Richard Russell Federal
   Building
75 Spring St S.W.
Atlanta GA 30303**

**USDA Forest Service,
PO Box 96090
Washington DC 20090
Phone: (800)283-CAMP**
Ask for a free list of campsites.

US Forest Service
US Forest Service/Alaska
PO Box 21628-RSc
Juneau AK 99802-1628

US Forest Service
PO Box 1279
Mountain View AR 72560

US Forest Service
608 West Commerce
Brownstown IN 47220

US Forest Service
Route 2 Box 268-a
Forest MS 39074

US Forest Service
Seeley Lake Ranger District
PO Box 717
Seeley Lake MT 59868

US Forest Pacific NW Region
PO Box 3623
Portland OR 97208

US STATE TOURIST OFFICES

Alabama Bureau of Tourism
532 South Perry Street
Montgomery AL 36130
(205)261-4169/
(800)392-8096

Alaska Division of Tourism
Box E
Juneau AK 99811
(907)465-2010

Arizona Tourism Office
1480 E. Bethany Home Road
Phoenix AZ 85014
(602)255-3618

Arkansas Department of Parks
One Capitol Mall
Little Rock AR 72201
(501)682-7777/(800)643-8383

California Tourism Office
1121 L Street
Sacramento CA 95814
(916)322-2882/(800)TO-CALIF

Colorado Tourism Board
Dept 124
Box 38700
Denver CO 80238
(303)592-5410/(800)265-6723

Connecticut Economic Devlpt.
210 Washington St, Rm 900
Hartford CT 06106
(203)566-3948/(800)243-1685

DC Visitors Association
1575 I St NW/Suite 250
Washington DC 20005
(202)787-7000

Delaware Tourism Office
99 Kings Highway,
Box 1401
Dover DE 19903
(302)736-4271/(800)441-8846

Florida Division of Tourism
126 Van Buren Street
Tallahassee FL 32301
(904)487-1462

Georgia Department of Tourism
Box 1776
Atlanta GA 30301
(404)656-3590

Hawaii Visitors Bureau
2270 Kala Kaua Avenue
Honolulu HI 96800
(808)923-1811

Idaho Travel Council
State Capitol Building
Boise ID 83720
(208)334-2470/(800)635-7820

Illinois Travel Center
Department of Commerce
310 S. Michigan Avenue/#108
Chicago IL 60604
(312)793-2094/(800)223-0121

Indiana Department of Commerce
Tourist Development
1 North Capitol Street
Indianapolis IN 46204
(317)232-8860/(800)2-WANDER

Iowa Tourist Travel
600 East Court Avenue
Des Moines IA 50309
(515)281-3100/(800)345-IOWA

Kansas Department of Travel
400 West 8th Street/5th floor
Topeka KS 66603
(914)296-2009

Kentucky Dept. of Travel
2200 Capitol Plaza Tower
Frankfort KY 40601
(502)564-4930/(800)225-TRIP

Louisiana Office of Tourism
Box 94291
Baton Rouge LA 70804
(504)925-3860/(800)334-8626

Maine Division of Tourism
97 Winthrop Street
Hallowell ME 04347
(207)289-2423/(800)533-9595

Maryland Office of Tourism
45 Calvert Street
Annapolis MD 21401
(301)974-3519/(800)331-1750

Massachusetts Divn. of Tourism
100 Cambridge Street
Boston MA 02202
(617)727-3201/(800)942-MASS

Michigan Travel Bureau
Box 30226
Lansing MI 48909
(517)373-0670/(800)543-2YES

Minnesota Office of Tourism
250 Skyway Level
375 Jackson Street
St. Paul MN 55101
(612)296-5029/(800)328-1461

Mississippi Division of Tourism
1301 Walter Sillers Building
Box 849
Jackson MS 39025
(601)359-3426/(800)647-2290

Missouri Division of Tourism
Truman State Office Building
PO Box 1055
Jefferson City MO 65102
(314)751-4133

Montana Travel Division
1424 9th Avenue
Helena MT 59620
(406)444-2654/(800)541-1447

Nebraska Division of Tourism
301 Centennial Mall South
PO Box 94666
Lincoln NE 68509
(402)471-3794/(800)228-4307

Nevada Commission of Tourism
State Capitol Complex
Carson City NV 89710
(702)885-3636/(800)NEV-ADA8

New Hampshire Vacation Travel
PO Box 856
Concord NH 03301
(603)271-2665

New Jersey Office of Tourism
CN-826
20 West State Street
Trenton NJ 08625
(609)292-2470/(800)JER-SEY7

New Mexico Tourism
Joseph Montoya Building
1100 St. Francis Drive
Santa Fe NM 87503
(505)827-0291/(800)545-2040

New York Division of Tourism
One Commerce Plaza
Albany NY 12245
(518)474-4116/(800)CALL-NYS

North Carolina Tourism Division
430 Salisbury Street
Box 25249
Raleigh NC 27611
(919)733-4171/(800)-VIS-ITNC

North Dakota Tourism Division
Liberty Memorial Building
Capitol Grounds
Bismarck ND 58505
(701)224-2525/(800)472-2100

Ohio Department of Tourism
Box 1001
Columbus OH 43266
(614)466-8844/(800)BUC-KEYE

Oklahoma Tourism Department
505 Will Rogers Building
Oklahoma City OK 73105
(405)521-2406/(800)652-6552

Oregon Division of Tourism
539 Cottage Street NE
Salem OR 97310
(503)378-3451/(800)547-7842

Pennsylvania Travel Department
416 Forum Building
Harrisburg PA 17120
(717)787-5453/(800)VIS-ITPA

Rhode Island Tourism
7 Jackson Walkway
Providence RI 02903
(401)277-2601/(800)556-2484

South Carolina Dept. of Parks,
Recreation & Tourism
Box 71
Columbia SC 29202
(803)734-0122

South Dakota Tourism
Capitol Lake Plaza
711 Wells Avenue
Pierre SD 57501
(605)773-3301/(800)843-8000

Tennessee Dept. of Tourism
Box 23170
Nashville TN 37202
(615)741-2158

Texas Travel Information
Box 5064
Austin TX 78763
(512)462-9191

Utah Travel Council
Council Hall
Capital Hill
Salt Lake City UT 84114
(801)533-5681

Vermont Travel Division
134 State Street
Montpelier VT 05602
(802)828-3236

Virginia Division of Tourism
Suite 500
202 West 9th Street
Richmond VA 23219
(804)786-2951/(800)VIS-ITVA

Washington State Tourism
101 General Admin. Bldg
Olympia WA 98504
(206)753-5600/(800)544-1800

West Virginia Tourism Office
State Capitol Complex
Charleston WV 25305
(304)348-2286/(800)CAL-LWVA

Wisconsin Division of Tourism
123 West Washington Avenue
PO Box 7606
Madison WI 53707
(608)266-2161/(800)432-TRIP

Wyoming Travel Commission
Frank Norris Travel Center
I-25 & College Drive,
Cheyenne WY 82002-0660
(307)777-7777/(800)225-5996

USA TERRITORIES

American Samoa Government
Office of Tourism
PO Box 1147
Pago Pago AS 96799
(684)633-5187

Guam Visitors Bureau
Pale San Vitores Road
PO Box 3520
Agana GU 96910
Phone: (671)646-5278

Marianas Visitors Bureau
PO Box 861
Saipan, CM,
Mariana Islands 96950
(670)234-8327

Puerto Rico Tourism Company
PO Box 125268
Miami FL 33102-5268
(212)541-6630/(800)223-6530

US Virgin Islands
Division of Tourism
Box 6400, VITIA
Charlotte Amalie,
St. Thomas, USVI 00801
(809)774-8784/(800)372-8784

VOLUNTEER OPENINGS

Alabama Horseshoe Bend
National Military Park
Route 1, Box 103
Daviston AL 36256

Alaska Parks & Outdoor Dept.
PO Box 107001-HO
Anchorage AK 99510

Arizona State Parks
800 West Washington #415
Phoenix AZ 85007

Arkansas Hot Springs
National Park
PO Box 1860
Hot Springs AR 71902

Colorado Divn Parks & Recn
Metro Regional Office
13787 S Highway 85
Littleton CO 80125

DC Parks & History Association
PO Box 40060
Washington DC 20016

DC Potomac Appalachian Trail
1718 N St NW
Washington DC 20036

Florida Park Service
Parks & Recreation
3900 Commonwealth Blvd
Room 525
Tallahassee FL 32399

Georgia Cumberland Island
National Seashore
PO Box 806
St Marys GA 31558

Hawaii Volcanoes National Park
PO Box 52 HI
Volcanoes NP HI 96718

Idaho Dept Parks & Recreation
Statehouse Mall
Boise ID 83720

Kansas Dept of Wildlife & Parks
Route 2, Box 54-a
Pratt KS 67124

Kentucky Parks
TVA Land Between Lakes
100 Van Morgan Drive
Golden Pont KY 42231

LA Kisatchie National Forest
Caney Ranger District
PO Box 479
Homer LA 71040

Maryland Parks
Antietam National Battlefield
PO Box 159
Sharpsburg MD 21782

Michigan Dept Natural Resources
Stevens T Mason Bldg
Lansing MI 48909

Missouri National Parks
Mark Twain National Forest
Rte 1, PO Box 182, Hwy 19
North Winona MO 65588

Nebraska National Parks
Scotts Bluff National Monument
PO Box 427
Gerin NE 69341

Nevada National Parks
Lake Mead Natl Recreation Area
601 Nevada Highway
Boulder City NV 89005

NH Division Parks & Recreation
105 Loudon Road
PO Box 856
Concord NH 03301

NY-NJ Trail Conference
232 Madison Avenue/Room 908
New York NY 10016

New Mexico State
Parks & Recreation
PO Box 1147
Santa Fe NM 87504

North Carolina National Forest
PO Box 2750
Asheville NC 28802

North Dakota Parks & Recreation
604 East Boulevard Avenue
Bismarck ND 58505-0662

Ohio Div Parks & Recreation
1952 Belcher/Bldg C-1
Columbus OH 43224

Oklahoma Parks
Chickasaw Natl Recreation Area
PO Box 201
Sulphur OK 73086

Oregon Parks
Pacific Crest Trail Conference
365 West 29th Avenue
Eugene OR 97405

Pennsylvania Natnl Parks
Erie National Wildlife Refuge
RD 1, Wood Duck Lane
Guys Mills, PA 16327

South Dakota
  Parks & Recreation Division
Anderson Building
Pierre SD 57501

Tennessee Parks
Shiloh National Military Park
PO Box 67
Shiloh TN 38376

Texas Aransas
National Wildlife Refuge
PO Box 100
Austwell TX 77950

Utah Canyonlands National Park
125 West 200 South
Moab UT 84532

Utah Divn of Parks & Recreation
1636 West North Temple
Salt Lake City UT 84116

Vermont State Parks
103 S Main Street
Waterbury VT 05676

Shenandoah National Park
Route 4, Box 348
Luray VA 22835

Virginia National Parks
Chincoteague National Wildlife
PO Box 62
Chincoteague VA 23336

Washington State
Parks & Recreation
7150 Cleanwater Lane KY-11
Olympia WA 98504

Wisconsin Apostle Islands
National Lakeshore
Route 1, Box 4
Bayfield WI 54814

Wyoming Bridger Teton
National Forest
Pinedale Ranger Station
PO Box 220
Pinedale WY 82941

198　*FAMILY TRAVEL*

INDEX

A
abroad, with children, 111, 116, 120
Acadia National Park, 38, 78
Adirondack Mountain Club, 60
Adventure Bound, 172
Africa, 46, 51, 72, 88, 114, 120, 122
Alaska Wilderness Sailing Safaris, 173
Alaska Wildland, 45
Alaska, 41, 151, 159, 167, 173
American Friends Service Cttee, 61
American Hiking Society, 62
American Inst. for Foreign Study, 114
America River Touring Assn., 174
American Wilderness Experience, 128
American Youth Hostels, 87
Amish, 18, 25, 17
Amsterdam, 101, 112
Appalachian Mountain Club, 63
archaeology, 67, 151, 158
Argentina, 102, 113
Arizona, 70, 123, 158, 165, 174
Arkansas, 70
art, 152, 156, 165
Asia, 72, 88, 114, 122
ASPIRE, 102
astronomy, 53, 91
Australia, 52, 88, 104, 114, 117, 120, 122, 162, 165
Austria, 84, 106, 108, 117, 150
Avenir Adventures, 115

B
Backpacker magazine, 21, 74
backpacking, 75, 91
Backroads, 84
Baja Expeditions, 175
bald eagles, 45
banjo, 155
barge tour, 162
Beds Abroad, 103
Belgium, 106, 109, 162
Belize, 117
Big Five Tours & Expeditions, 46
biking, 25, 73, 80, 95, 128, 160, 177
bird-watching, 48, 91, 117, 177, 181
blacksmithing, 151, 155
Bluffdale Vacation Farm, 22
boating, 153, 156, 157, 178, 179
Brazil, 47, 117
Buccholz, C. W., 93
Budapest, 108
budget, 5, 6
business, 104

C
California, 56, 70, 87, 89, 95, 97, 109, 123, 162
calligraphy, 156, 160
Campbell Folk School, 155
Canada, 84, 97, 100, 104, 168, 178
Canoe Country Escapes, 176

canoeing, 25, 53, 128, 160, 169, 176, 177, 184
Cape Cod National Seashore, 38, 87
Caribbean, 4, 100, 120, 122
cattle round-ups, 124, 125, 129, 131, 132, 133
Chatauqua Institution, 156
Cherokee, 164
Cheyenne River Ranch, 129
Chile, 102, 113
China, 114, 115, 165
City Slickers, 124
Colorado, 92, 95, 97, 109, 123, 124, 130, 132, 153, 158, 161, 172, 174, 182
    Dude & Guest Ranch, 130
Copper Mountain skiing, 148
coral reefs, 179
Cornell's Adult University, 157
Costa Rica, 43, 47, 51, 52, 88, 175
Country Inns Along the Trail, 85
cowboys, 123
Craftsbury Nordic Center, 86
Crested Butte skiing, 148
crocodiles, 47, 65
Crow Canyon Archaeological, 153, 158
Czechoslovakia, 108, 116

D
dancing, 124, 133, 151, 152, 155
Delaware Gap, 68
Denmark, 107, 112
Denver Museum Natural History, 159
Devils Tower Natl. Monument, 64
Diamond Peak skiing, 148
Dillman's Creative Workshops, 160
Dinosaur Discovery Expeditions, 161
dinosaurs, 151, 153, 161
disabilities, 119
dude ranches, 123-137
Dude Ranchers Association, 130
dulcimer, 151, 155

E
Ecotour Expeditions, 47
Ecuador, 47, 79, 90, 102, 113

educational, 42, 122, 151, 156
Egypt, 104
Elderhostel, 122
England, 97, 99, 107, 109, 120, 162
environment, 67, 68
Europe, 72, 84, 100, 101, 112, 114, 122, 150, 165
exchange, 97, 98, 99, 104, 105, 107

F
Faculty Exchange Center, 104
FamilyHostel, 111, 116
fiddle, 155
Fiji, 120
Finland, 120
First Aid, 37
fishing, 24, 25, 53, 54, 70, 117, 123, 128, 133, 153, 156, 177, 180, 181
Florida, 65, 97, 100, 109, 122, 165, 167
    Park Service, 65
Food First, 66
Forum Travel International, 117
France, 72, 95, 97, 102, 106, 108, 109, 112, 113, 114, 115, 117, 120, 150

G
Galapagos Islands, 44, 51, 52, 120
geology, 48, 173
Georgia, 164
Germany, 84, 97, 102, 106, 107, 108, 109, 113, 117, 122
Gibbons, Euell, 28
glaciers, 91, 173
golf, 153, 156, 157, 160
Grand Targhee skiing, 148
Grand Canyon, 78
grandparents, 42, 139, 151, 162, 163
Grandtravel, 162
Greece, 106, 115
Green Chimneys, 66
Gunflint Northwoods Outfitters, 177

H
Harvey's Mountain View Farm, 21
Hawaii, 52, 97, 104, 109, 120, 151, 165
High Island Guest Ranch, 131

hiking, 24, 25, 45, 54, 68, 73, 75, 85, 121, 123, 126, 238, 153, 157, 160, 177
Hong Kong, 107
horseriding, 24, 27, 28, 76, 92, 123, 125, 132, 133
Hostelling International, 87
House Exchange Program, 105
Houseboat Holidays, 178
icefishing, 123
Iceland, 107

I
Idaho, 80, 123, 174, 181 182
India, 90, 107, 115, 165
Indians, 131, 151, 164, 166, 176
Ingeberg Acres, 23
Inn at East Hill Farm, 24
Interhome, 106
International Workcamps, 72
Intervac US, 107
Iowa, 164
Ireland, 102, 117
Israel, 104, 113
    Kibbutz Hotels, 118
Italy, 102, 106, 109, 112, 150, 165

J
Jamaica, 100, 1113, 120
Journeys, 88
Journeys into American Indian Territory, 164

K
kayak, 54, 128, 160, 169, 175, 181
Kenya, 46, 52, 162, 184

L
languages, 121, 122, 151, 153, 157
llama, 76, 128, 166
London, 103, 105, 109

M
Marine Sciences Under Sail, 179
Massachusetts, 97, 109
Mexico, 100, 102, 116, 117, 120, 159, 175

Michel Farm Vacations, 25
Michigan, 146
Minnesota, 70, 167, 169, 176
Mobility International, 119
Montana, 123, 130
Montecito-Sequoia Nordic Ski, 89
moose, 84, 180, 177
mountain bikes, 80, 128
Mountain Dale Farm, 27
music, 151, 156
Myths and Mountains, 90

N
National Wildlife Federation, 42, 48
nature, 91, 117, 126, 155, 160
Nepal, 5, 79, 88, 90, 165
Netherlands, 72, 98, 106, 107, 109, 111, 116, 162
Nevada, 158
New Zealand, 52, 88, 104, 120
New Jersey, 68
New York, 60, 68, 72, 97, 109, 123, 151, 152, 162, 183
New Hampshire, 78
New Mexico, 158
North Carolina, 56, 67, 70, 94, 155
    National Forest, 67

O
O.A.R.S., 180
Okeanos Ocean Research Fndn, 49
Oklahoma, 151, 164
Olde Fogie Farm, 28
Olympic Park Institute, 42, 50
Oregon, 91, 174, 180
Overseas Adventure Travel, 51

P
Pacific Northwest Field Seminars, 91
painting, 153, 160
Pennsylvania, 17, 18, 68, 87, 123, 183
photography, 48, 53, 91, 155, 160, 165
Pocono Environmental Education, 68
prehistoric, 67
Purgatory Durango skiing, 148

Q
quilting, 151, 154, 155

R
Rascals in Paradise, 120
Redwood National Park, 69
river-rafting, 92, 117, 128, 168, 172, 174, 180, 181, 182, 183, 184
Roads Less Traveled, 92
Rocky Mountain Cattle Moovers, 132
    National Park, 38, 74
    Nature Assn., 93
    River Tours, 181
Russia, 72, 113, 121
Russian Homestay, 121

S
sailing, 128, 153, 173
Schweitzer skiing, 148
Sierra Club, 56, 70, 78, 94
skating, 24, 89
skiing, crosscountry, 24, 25, 73, 85, 86, 89, 128
    downhill, 139-148
    Europe, 150
sleigh riding, 121
Smithsonian National Assocs., 165
snowmobiling, 123, 128
snorkeling, 54, 160, 175, 179
Spain, 97, 102, 104, 106, 107, 109, 116
Special Expeditions, 166
Steamboat skiing, 148
Sweden, 107
Switzerland, 98, 107, 108, 112, 116, 150

T
Tandem Touring Company, 95
Tanzania, 46, 52, 160
tennis, 24, 153, 156, 157, 160
Texas, 123, 130
Thailand, 90, 109
Tibet, 90, 165

U
University of New Hampshire, 111
Untours Idyll Ltd, 108

Utah, 92, 123, 161, 168, 172, 174, 180, 182

V
Vacation Exchange Club, 98, 109
Venezuela, 47, 117
Venice, 113, 165
Vermont, 56, 71, 80
    State Parks, 71
Villas & Apartments Abroad, 109
Virgin Islands National Park, 38
Volunteers for Peace, 72

W
Washington DC, 151, 162
Washington State, 91, 94
water-skiing, 25, 133, 160
Western River Expeditions, 182
whalewatching, 42, 49, 54, 169, 175
Whitewater Challenges, 183
Wilderness Trails Ranch, 133
Wildland Adventures, 52
windsurfing, 117
Wisconsin, 123, 153, 160
woodworking, 151, 155
World Learning, 122
Wyoming, 70, 124, 129, 130, 161, 180

Y
Yellowstone Natl. Park, 38, 53, 159
Yellowstone Institute, 53

Z
Zimbabwe, 107
Zoar Outdoor, 184
Zoetic Research, 54

202 *FAMILY TRAVEL*

BPP Travel Resource Guides

If you enjoyed FAMILY TRAVEL, take a look at other BPP Travel Resource Guides from Blue Penguin, designed for aware and informed travelers.

TRAVEL AND LEARN: The New Guide to Educational Travel 1992-1993 by Evelyn Kaye. Describes more than 1,500 exciting learning vacations around the world on the arts, archaeology, language, music, ecology, human relations, and outdoor adventures. 350 pages, illustrations, index. $23.95. ISBN 0-9626231-2-1. LC 90-81540

> "For an inveterate traveler, this book is perfect." *Lewiston Tribune, Idaho.*
>
> "A handy and concise reference guide to educational vacation programs. Clearly written and well organized. Good browsing for travelers." *American Library Association Booklist.*
>
> "The range of topics is amazing. You can cruise the Atlantic, brush up on your Japanese in Tokyo, visit Alaska, China and Australia, or read Shakespeare's plays at an English university." *Source Travel Newsletter, California.*

ECO-VACATIONS: Enjoy Yourself and Save the Earth by Evelyn Kaye. Hundreds of unique environmental trips offered by 81 museums, ecological organizations and non-profit institutions including the American Museum of Natural History, Habitat for Humanity, National Audubon Society, and Student Conservation Association. 242 pages, illustrations index. $22.50. ISBN 0-9626231-1-3. LC 91-070296.

> "The single most comprehensive source of information on ecological tours." *New York Times, Travel.*
>
> "A marvelously well organized and simple way to find out just which ecological vacation is best for any particular reader. It's exactly what you need to have a fulfilling vacation and save the earth." *Travelwriter Marketletter.*
>
> "Heartily recommended for singles looking for short or long retreats. Mention the book to your library too." *Pat Kite, columnist.*

....

BOOKS ORDER FORM

Please send me:

_____ copy/ies FAMILY TRAVEL $19.95 + $2.55 shipping ($22.50)
_____ copy/ies TRAVEL AND LEARN $23.95 + $2.55 shipping ($26.50)
_____ copy/ies ECO-VACATIONS $22.50 + $2.50 shipping ($25.00)

Enclosed is my check to Blue Penguin for $_____
Charge my credit card Visa/Mastercard#_____ Exp.date_____

Name...

Address..

....
Phone:...
SEND TO: BPP, 3031 Fifth Street, Boulder, CO. 80304. (303)449-8474
TO ORDER TODAY CALL TOLL FREE 1-800-800-8147